Driven to Espresso

Drive-through coffee stands in the Northwest

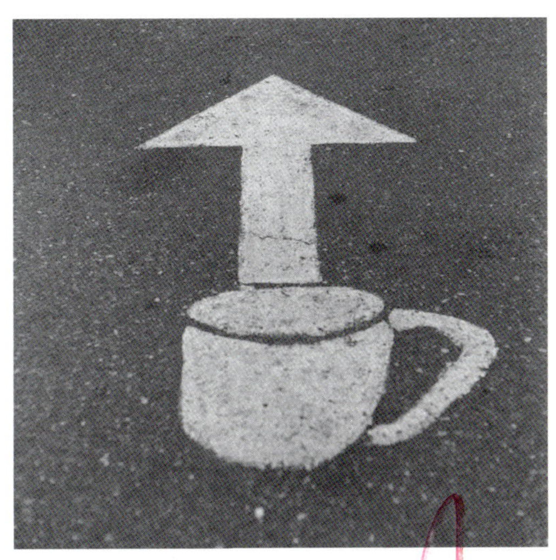

Ray Weisgerber

1 by 1 Publishing

1 by 1 Publishing, P.O. Box 1391, Edmonds, Washington 98020-1391, info@1by1publishing.com

ISBN: 9780615230894

Library of Congress Control Number: 2008909855

Printed in China

Cover photo: Hotspot Coffee, Arlington, Washington

Contents

Foreword

I remember driving to Seattle about 20 years ago and seeing my first espresso drive-through. It was owned by a good friend of mine, and although his location was on the wrong side of the road (the evening-drive side) and his operation was difficult to access, he still had lines of cars on both sides of what today would be considered a coffee shack.

Within a year of that introduction, coffee drive-throughs started showing up everywhere on the West Coast—after Washington, the concept moved south to Oregon and then to California.

There are several reasons this idea spread as quickly as it did. For one thing, specialty coffee became a daily habit for those living in the Northwest. No longer was stale convenience-store coffee acceptable. Once consumers tasted great coffee, there was no turning back. But why did the coffee drive-through really explode so quickly? One word—*convenience*. No longer did the mother with two children in her SUV need to park and get her family out of the car and into a coffee shop to get her daily fix. And often there were menu options for her children as well.

The one thing most of us lack in today's society is time, so we seek convenience to give us more of it. The coffee drive-through satisfies both of these needs.

With this book, Ray shows us the creativity of the independent coffee entrepreneur. In the beginning, many operations were tool sheds with a service window cut in the side, and others were simply glorified carts with a roof. Now 20 years later, drive-throughs serve a wide array of menu items and are sophisticated buildings with styling and design worthy of a national fast-food chain.

This book serves as an inspiration and historical snapshot of the creativity of this significant niche in the specialty coffee industry.

Bruce Milletto
President, Bellissimo Coffee InfoGroup
Founder, The American Barista & Coffee School

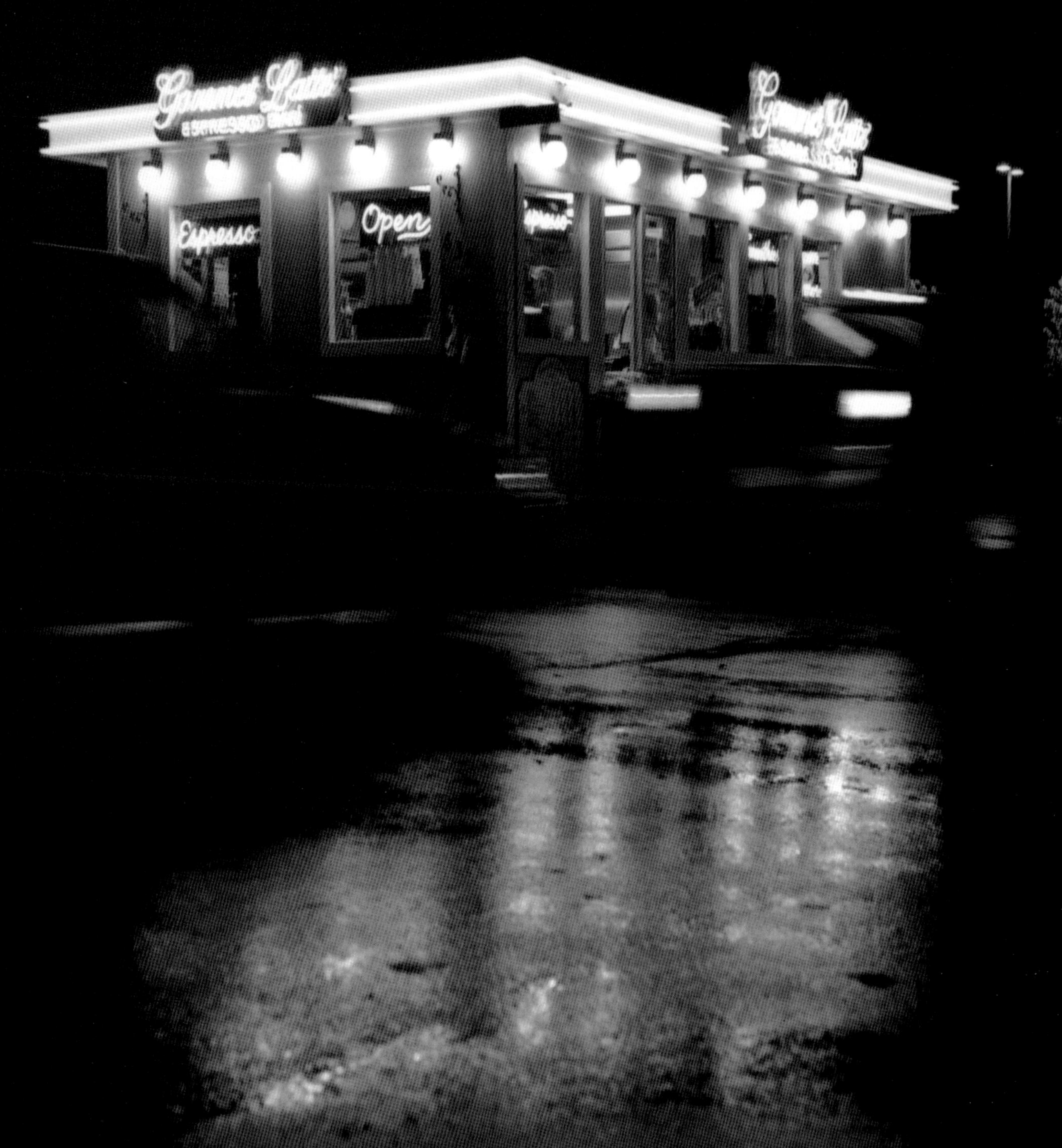
Espresso
Open

Introduction

It's raining again.

I'm already running late for my nine o'clock meeting, and I have a good hour-and-a-half drive to Bellingham ahead of me. Fortunately, I have the drive down cold, and northbound traffic from Seattle should be minimal, so there's enough time for the one stop I must make before the freeway: this morning cries out for a double-tall-nonfat-mocha-no-whip.

When I pull into the Gourmet Latte lot, I'm third in line. Well, fifth, if you count the cars on both sides of this drive-through espresso stand. It won't take long, and while I'm waiting I can clear out my cup holder. The baristas at Gourmet Latte are good at their jobs: fast, courteous, and they make a great cup of coffee. They're not bad-looking, either!

It is no great secret that coffee is a big deal in Seattle. Ask anyone from another part of the world what they know about Seattle, and they'll tell you that it rains in Seattle and people there drink a lot of coffee. I've always assumed that the two are related.

In his 2005 book, *A History of the World in 6 Glasses,* Tom Standage offers another interesting correlation. "The original coffeehouse culture is echoed perhaps best in Internet cafes and wireless-Internet hot spots that facilitate the caffeine-fueled exchange of information, and in coffee-shop chains that are used as ad hoc offices and meeting rooms by mobile workers. Is it any surprise that the current center of coffee culture, the city of Seattle, home to the Starbucks coffeehouse chain, is also where some of the world's largest software and Internet firms are based? Coffee's association with innovation, reason, and networking—plus a dash of revolutionary fervor—has a long pedigree."

For whatever reason, Seattle consumes far more specialty coffee than the average American city, and from Seattle the culture spreads outward—the whole Pacific Northwest is addicted to espresso. The outskirts don't have as many coffeehouses as the urban hubs, but in virtually any populated area, big or small, it's

◂ *Gourmet Latte, Lynnwood, Washington*

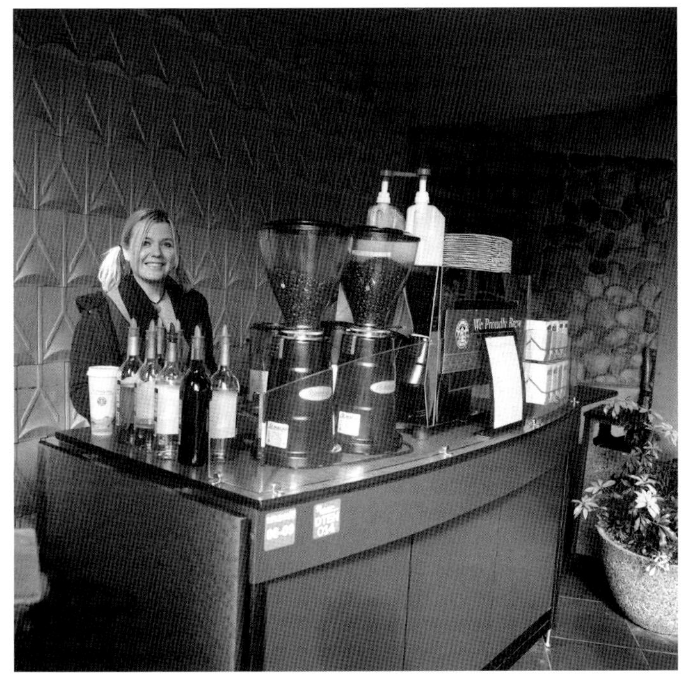

Angela Kiel at the Edgewater Hotel's espresso cart, Seattle

not hard to find expertly-drawn espresso at a convenient location. The further you get from urban and suburban neighborhoods, the density of true coffeehouses decreases, while drive-through espresso stands increase in number. They seem to be at every intersection along the main arterials and at every freeway exit.

King County, where Seattle is located, amended a development code in 1994 to accommodate espresso drive-throughs. In the new code they are only required to have room for three cars in each lane (other fast-food restaurants need seven), *if three or more other such establishments exist within a quarter-mile radius.* Three or more espresso drive-through stands within a quarter mile of each other? Apparently King County realizes that finding that level of concentration is not altogether unlikely.

Although no one can say exactly how many espresso drive-throughs exist in the Northwest, Washington and Oregon easily have as many as a thousand combined. If you need a caffeine fix and don't want to get out of your car, this is definitely the place to be. Even though drive-through espresso is growing in other parts of the county faster than it is here, they have a lot of catching up to do.

With so many stands built over a 20-year period, the differences in their design and construction demonstrate an evolution that actually started with sidewalk carts in the 1980s. These became ubiquitous in front of department stores, grocery stores, and gas stations; on sidewalks and jogging trails; and just about anywhere with a regular flow of pedestrians. Various sources trace the appearance of Seattle's first espresso cart to 1980, crediting either Craig "Cappuccino Craig" Donarum, located under the monorail, or to Nordstrom, which placed a cart on the sidewalk in front of its flagship store that year. In any case, Nordstrom evidently has the oldest continuously operated sidewalk espresso cart business in Seattle. (Donarum sold his operator's license less than a year later to Chuck Beek, who still operates a sidewalk coffee bar on Pike Street.)

In the espresso cart heyday of the 1980s, a fully equipped espresso cart cost about $6,000 at Costco. Add coffee, a portable water supply, and a few other basic ingredients, and anyone was ready to "pull shots." Passionate baristas who found a good location quickly became successful. Well, busy, at least.

But as more and more coffeehouses opened—Howard Schultz's first espresso cafe, Il Giornale, opened in 1985—carts began to disappear. Sitting in a warm, dry place with background music, art on the walls, and maybe even a comfortable chair was a lot more pleasant than waiting on the pavement in the rain for a cappuccino. Besides, what could you do with your laptop at a sidewalk cart?

As for drive-throughs, they are obviously more convenient for someone in a car, where, let's face it, most Americans tend to log a lot of time. Drive-through espresso stands began to appear around 1990, catering to a more mobile suburban customer. The first ones were typically conversions from other types of buildings, trailers, or simple garden sheds. Soon after those initial conversions, newer ones were planned and constructed specifically for use as espresso drive-throughs. Today, some entrepreneurs erect elaborately styled drive-throughs with architectural significance to make their businesses stand out.

All of these types of drive-throughs are still doing business throughout the Northwest. Converted trailers, tool sheds, abandoned gas stations, and other building conversions remain a relatively low-cost way to get into the drive-through espresso business. With a small financial investment and the selection of a good location, an espresso drive-through can pull in $400 to $1,000 in coffee sales every single day of the year.

In the late-1990s, a lot of people came to realize that potential existed, and drive-through espresso stands took off like a Boeing jet—it was a small-business notion ideally suited to the independent spirit of America. "There is so much opportunity in this industry that it's frightening," says Bruce Milletto, owner of Bellissimo Coffee InfoGroup and a leader in the specialty-coffee industry.

After the early building conversions showed drive-through owners the potential profit in the business, a growing number realized they could spend a little more money on their locations and gain more operational efficiency and, therefore, even more profit. Today many drive-throughs are designed and constructed from the ground up specifically for this purpose. They have a foundation, plumbing, and a paved parking lot, and consequently look more like a conventional business, albeit a tiny one.

Building from the ground up means the owner has a better chance of satisfying those pesky bureaucrats at city hall. The typical drive-through owner must now deal with the local building department, health department, sign commission, department of transportation, utility commission, license bureau, and fire marshal. No longer able to fly under the radar, this new generation of drive-throughs must give the appearance of permanence, even if their above-ground, wooden foundations can be picked up and moved somewhere else.

With new drive-throughs always opening, and some owners adopting more sophisticated business practices—such as barista training programs, improved location analysis, and careful attention to the quality of the product—the competition in this field is growing. So is the influence of chain ownership: Christian Kar, owner of Espresso Connection drive-throughs, started with a cart, then opened a drive-through stand, and eventually expanded to 18 locations. He also owns Silver Cup Coffee, a coffee-roasting and equipment sales company, and The Coffee Coach Advantage, a training organization for espresso-industry professionals. Claiming he has made a profit nearly every year since his first espresso cart operation, he estimates his coffee companies have grossed over $65 million in sales since.

But independents still dominate the field, and despite the proliferation of permanent-looking drive-through stands and the increasing use of architectural finesse, many older, conversion-style drive-throughs don't seem to be hurting. The Northwest just has so many serious caffeine addicts, and a stand's location and the quality of its drinks are, of course, the most important factors in achieving success.

To me, the adapters who convert simple buildings into drive-through espresso stands embody the quintessential American small businessperson. While many of these smaller operations can hold their own or even thrive, the industry is not without its casualties. It's not difficult to find a dark and deserted drive-through

Espresso Connection,
Mill Creek, Washington

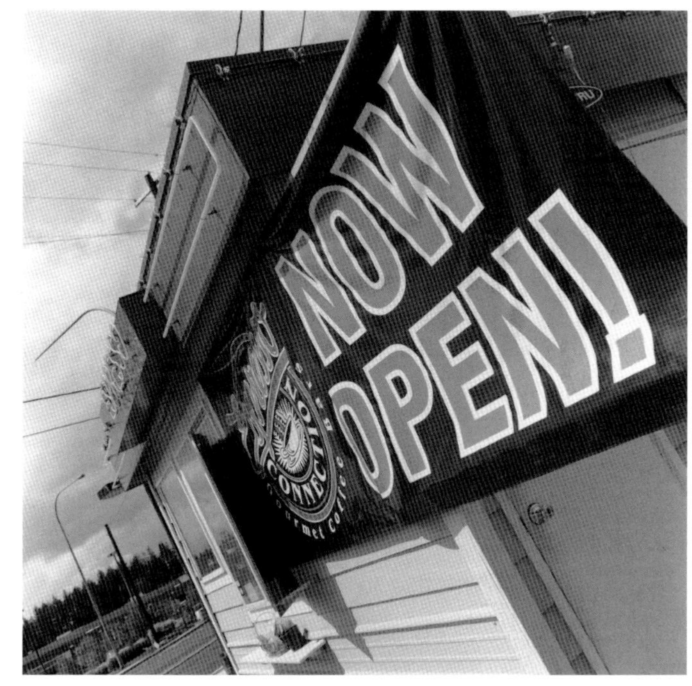

along a suburban street or highway, sometimes with weeds sticking through the pavement and a weathered "For Sale" sign in the window. I gaze at the small buildings or trailers and wonder if they will be reborn. And I try to imagine the reasons for their abandonment—perhaps the location was not ideal, product quality was not a priority, the lease was not renewable, or the owner's involvement proved insufficient.

Many of these drive-through buildings are more-or-less portable and, in fact, often get physically moved to a better location. Or a *different* one in any case—I visited one stand that had been moved exactly one parking lot away, only to have a new drive-through sprout up in its original location. They were so close I could flip a coffee cup lid from one to the other.

Drive-throughs without wheels or with more solid foundations are typically left standing on the site and sold to another spirited entrepreneur. A new name, a new brand of coffee, a fresh paint job, a different menu, and redesigned decorations nailed to the siding, and a whole new business is born. Maybe the new one will fare better. Perhaps, if the owners place a sandwich board or lighted marquee near the curb with messages such as, "Mad Mondays—All Drinks $2," or "Twice the Caffeine as Starbucks."

Or they might try a technique older than coffee itself: more and more baristas are wearing less and less. A *Seattle Times* article in January 2007 publicized the phenomenon of "sexpresso" drive-throughs that

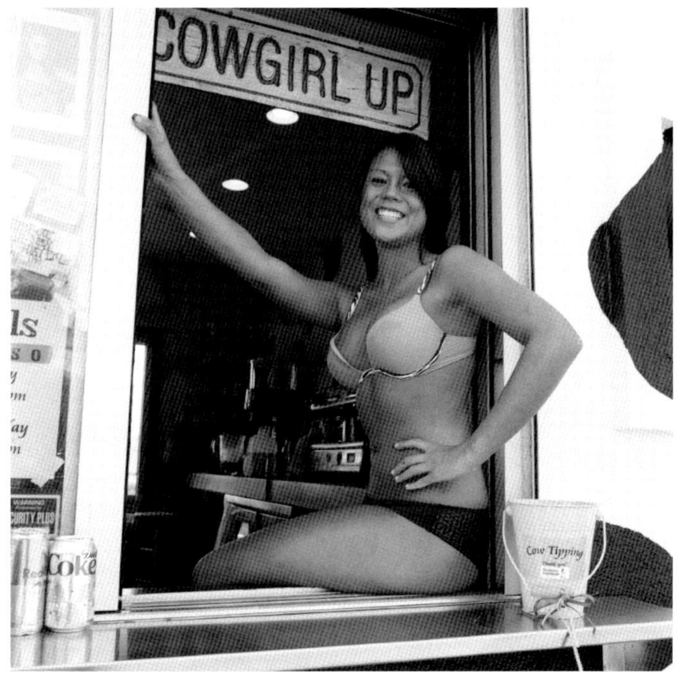

Kim Schmidt, barista at Cowgirls Espresso in Auburn, Washington

employ bikini- or negligee-clad baristas and even an occasional topless barista. Ever since then, a steady number of espresso drive-throughs have adopted this tactic to attract more customers (more men, anyway) to their windows.

As the sophistication of the drive-through espresso stand continues, more professionals such as architects and branding consultants are making their mark in the industry. Following the advice of these highly paid experts, serious investors can spend $500,000 or more on drive-through espresso operations that feature taller buildings; high-end design work on logos, menus, and signage; landscaping; and uniformed baristas. Many of the fancier operations are part of a chain, but even some independently owned stands sport a polished style all their own.

Scott Olson of Go Architects in the Puget Sound region, who designs drive-throughs for clients coast-to-coast, explains that a drive-through business can best survive if it has an assertive visual presence. Added height improves visibility for a small drive-through stand that doesn't have the overall size to draw attention, considering all the other typical surrounding visual distractions, so Olson designs drive-throughs that have two stories.

Ed Arvidson, another consultant to the industry, tells his clients that extra height can be practical as well. Having room to store coffee cups directly above the workspace, for example, improves the barista's ability to produce more drinks in less time. With a background as a manager in the fast-food industry, Arvidson designs and sells drive-through floor plans that maximize efficiency for his customers.

Outbuildings, sometimes as large as the drive-through itself, can be another way to add space. Some tool shed-conversion drive-throughs have two or more other sheds on their lots, just for supplies. It can become a village of little sheds!

Entrepreneurs who hope to grow beyond one or two locations can develop their business plans with the help of consultants such as Lon LaFlamme of The Brand Coaches in Sumner, Washington. LaFlamme advises his clients that the days of converted sheds are over, and that their business must exude corporate confidence when a potential customer spots their stand along a busy street.

The stakes are indeed higher these days. In 1990, an initial investment of around $10,000 was sufficient to open a drive-through espresso stand. That figure grew to well over $50,000 by 2001, and now some businesses invest $500,000 or more to get in the drive-through espresso game. This equates to selling a lot of triple-shot-soy-almond-lattes. In fact, successful drive-throughs now sell $300,000 worth of coffee drinks annually, and in some cases much more.

According to LaFlamme, operating a successful drive-through espresso stand in the future will be daunting, to say the least. On his website he posts a prophecy almost as scary as that from a fire-and brimstone preacher: "Dive deep into today's drive-through game or face certain death."

Regardless of how elaborate the new structures get and how much the competition increases, the fact that many drive-through espresso stands built 15 years ago are still booming and yielding substantial returns attracts enthusiastic newcomers to the business each year. Since the average cost to make a brewed cup of specialty coffee is 40 cents, and the average customer pays $1.85 for that cup, plenty of 10-foot by 10-foot drive-throughs continue to pull in enough revenue to convince their plucky independent owners to stick it out a little longer. The question is, how much longer? Will corporate tactics eventually force out the small, no-frills locations? It seems reasonable to assume that after big business runs the numbers, it will swallow up independent espresso stands just as it has the neighborhood pizza joints, groceries, hardware stores, and bookstores.

But maybe not; I'm hedging my bets for several reasons. First of all, coffee (espresso especially) attracts passionate consumers who decide for themselves which stand has the best product, regardless of the style of its building and signage, and this attitude has sustained small coffee businesses for centuries. Second, it takes only about 200 cups of coffee a day for a small espresso stand to turn a profit. Third, even though large corporations have moved into neighborhoods that were previously served exclusively by local businesses, there are still some local merchants who remain and thrive, becoming landmarks in their communities by sustaining the important qualities that made them popular in the first place. And finally, the dream of operating a small, profitable business out of a 100-square-foot building is so tempting to so many that there will likely be a supply of eager participants for a long time to come.

Ray Weisgerber

Buzzin' Bob's, Shoreline, Washington

Bob Tonning's cart stood in front of a convenience store at 175th Street NW and Aurora Avenue North for many years. When I spoke with him on a hot July morning in 2005, he told me his business was not doing well. He said the summer months were never his busiest, but this was the worst he could remember. One of the things that had kept him in business, at least so far, was that there were no other espresso businesses on that busy corner. Bob figured he would wait until the cooler months and see if it picked up. If not, he thought he'd have to pack up his syrups and go home. A few months later, the cart was gone.

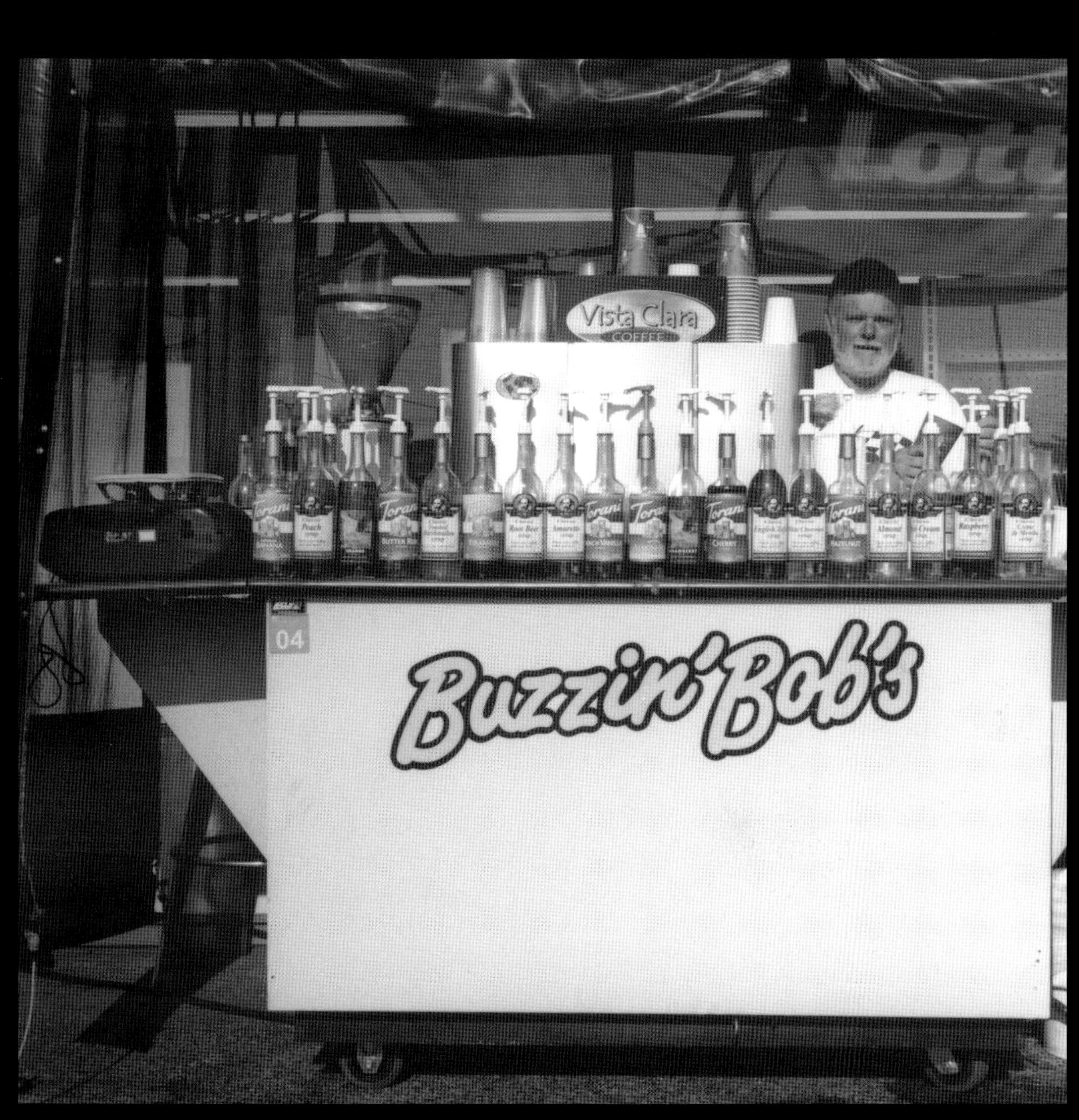
Vista Clara
COFFEE
Torani
Peach
Root Beer
Amaretto
Cherry
Hazelnut
Almond
Raspberry
04
Buzzin' Bob's

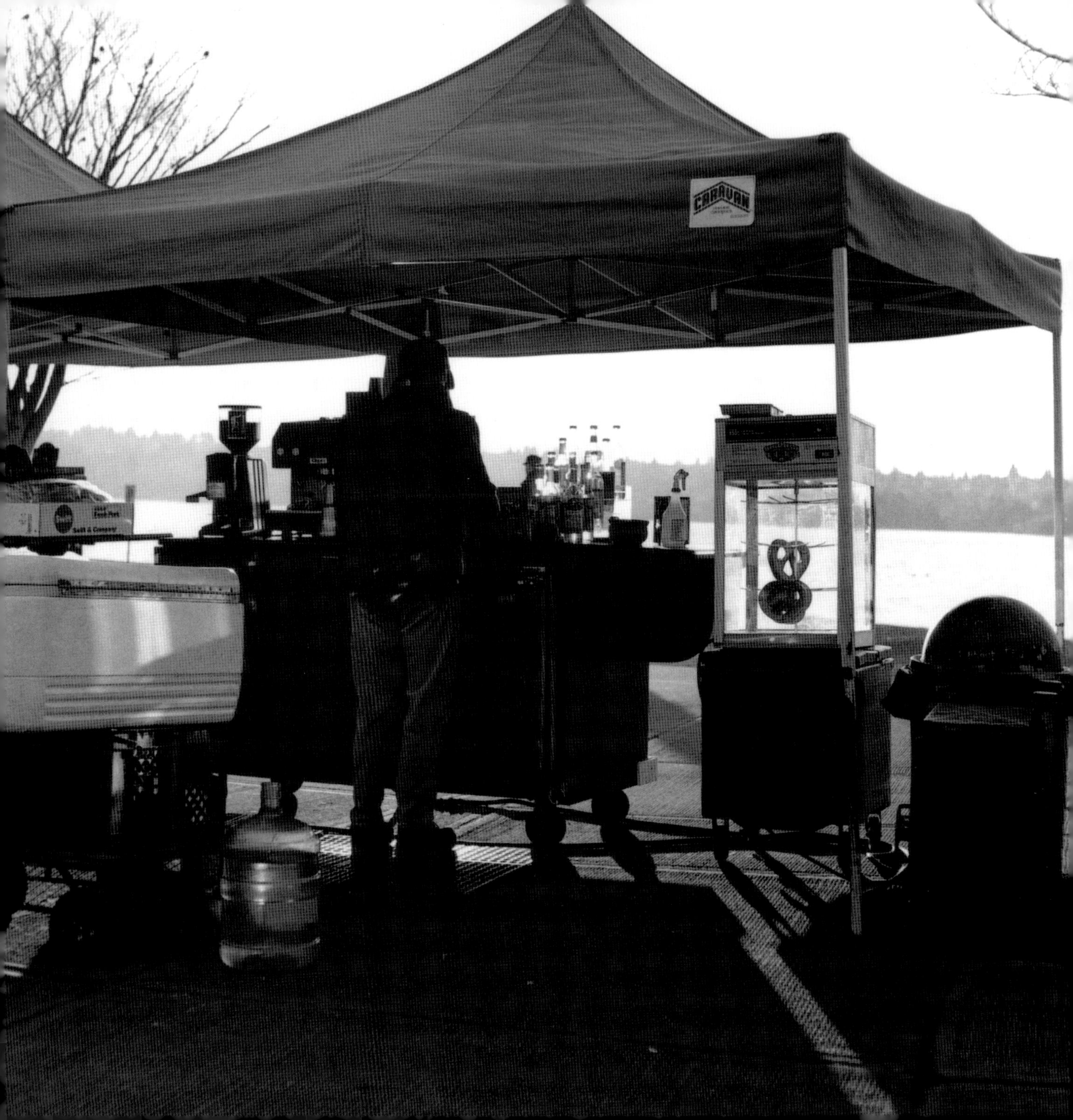
CARAVAN

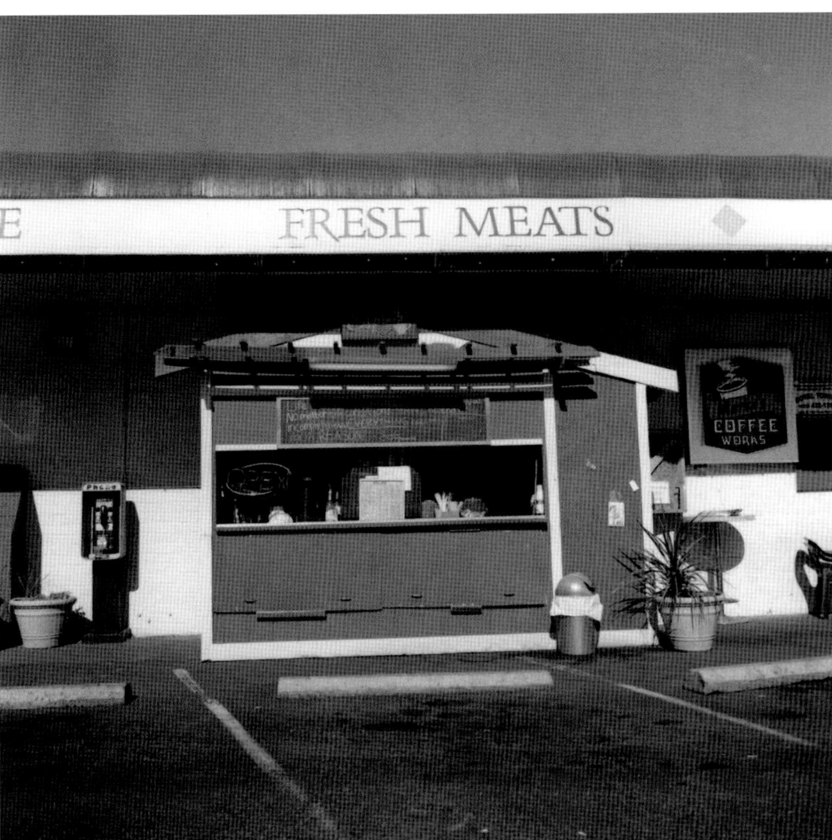

▲ *Marka's Coffee Works, Maple Valley, Washington*

◂ *The Green Lake espresso cart, Seattle, Washington*

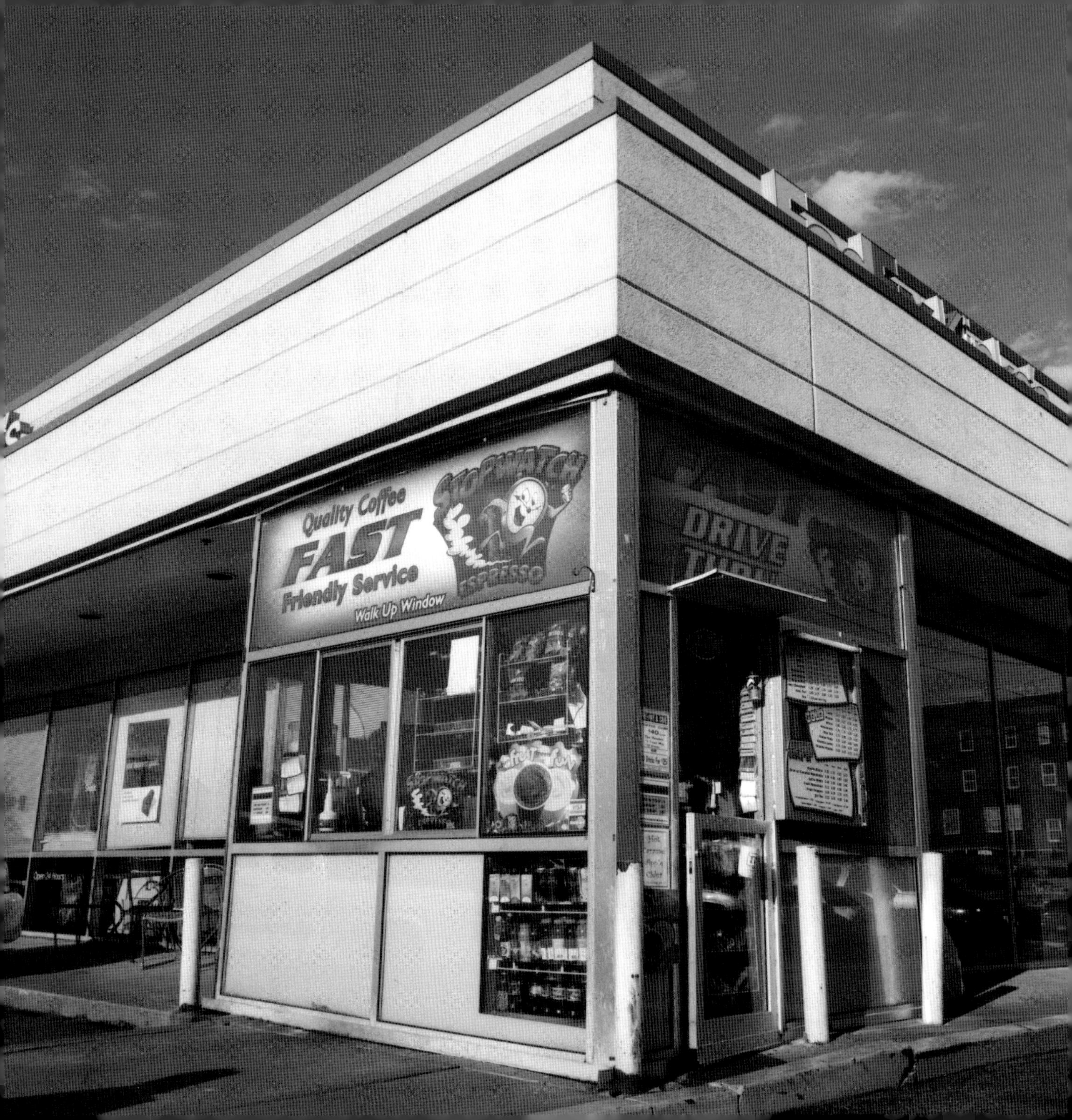
Quality Coffee
FAST
Friendly Service
Walk Up Window
STOPWATCH
ESPRESSO
DRIVE

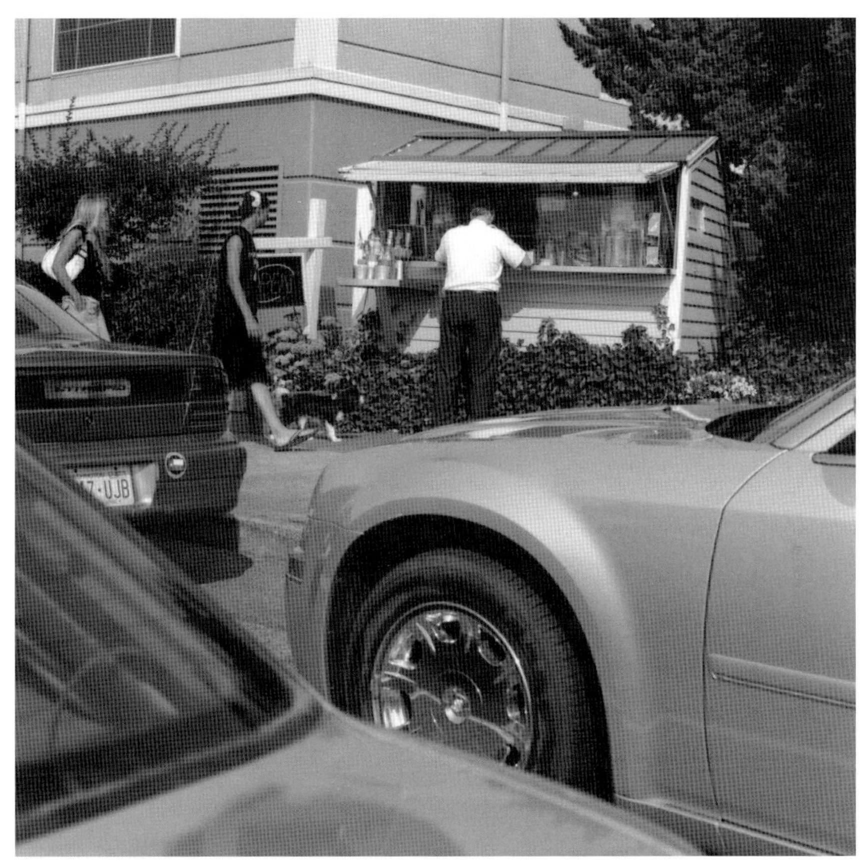

▲ *Terminal Caffeine, Edmonds, Washington*

◂ *Stop Watch Espresso, Lynnwood, Washington*

Espresso Chalet, Index, Washington

Mark "Espressomeister" Klein and his wife, Sandy, have operated this espresso stand in a converted 1961 "Li'l Loafer" Aristocrat Travel Trailer along U.S. Route 2 since 1992. Located far from urban surroundings on one of the mountainous routes between western and eastern Washington, the Espresso Chalet attracts mostly hikers and skiers. Besides its unique look, the business stands out for the menu choices the Kleins offer, including 170 flavors for espresso drinks or milk-shakes, and 11 different kinds of milk.

Espresso Chalet is sometimes referred to as "Bigfoot Espresso," undoubtedly because of its large, carved statue of that legendary creature, not to mention the adjacent Bigfoot Museum, which is located in a Quonset hut that was used for a location shot in the 1987 film *Harry and the Hendersons*.

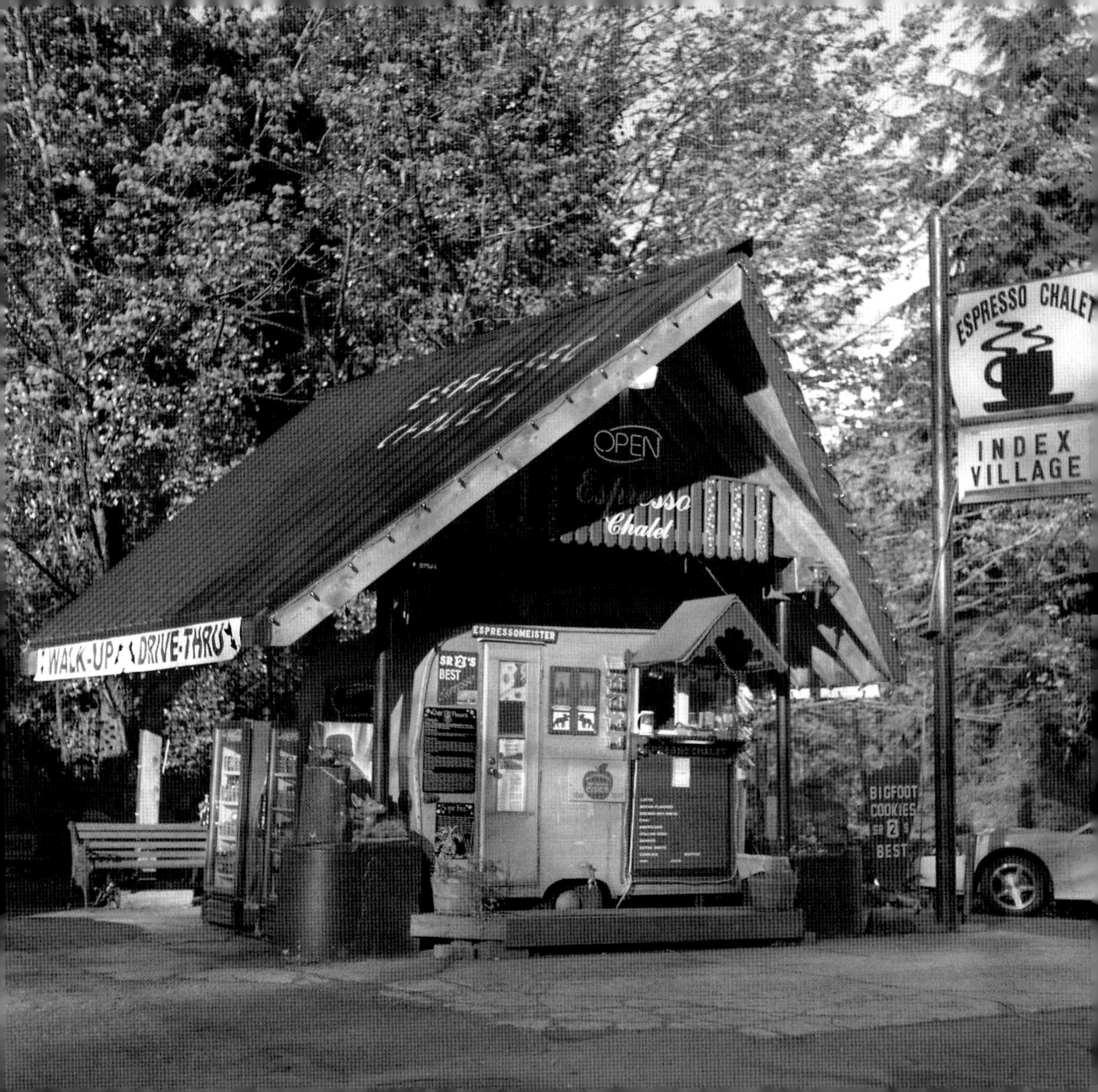
ESPRESSO CHALET
INDEX
VILLAGE
OPEN
Espresso
Chalet
WALK-UP
DRIVE-THRU
ESPRESSOMEISTER
SR 2'S
BEST
BIGFOOT
COOKIES
SR 2 'S
BEST

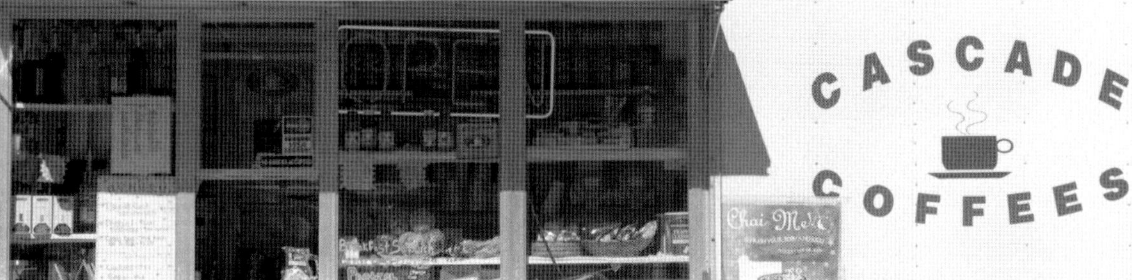
Cascade Coffees
Espresso
PASTRIES • MUFFINS • BREAKFAST SANDWICHES
CASCADE
COFFEES
Cascade Coffees

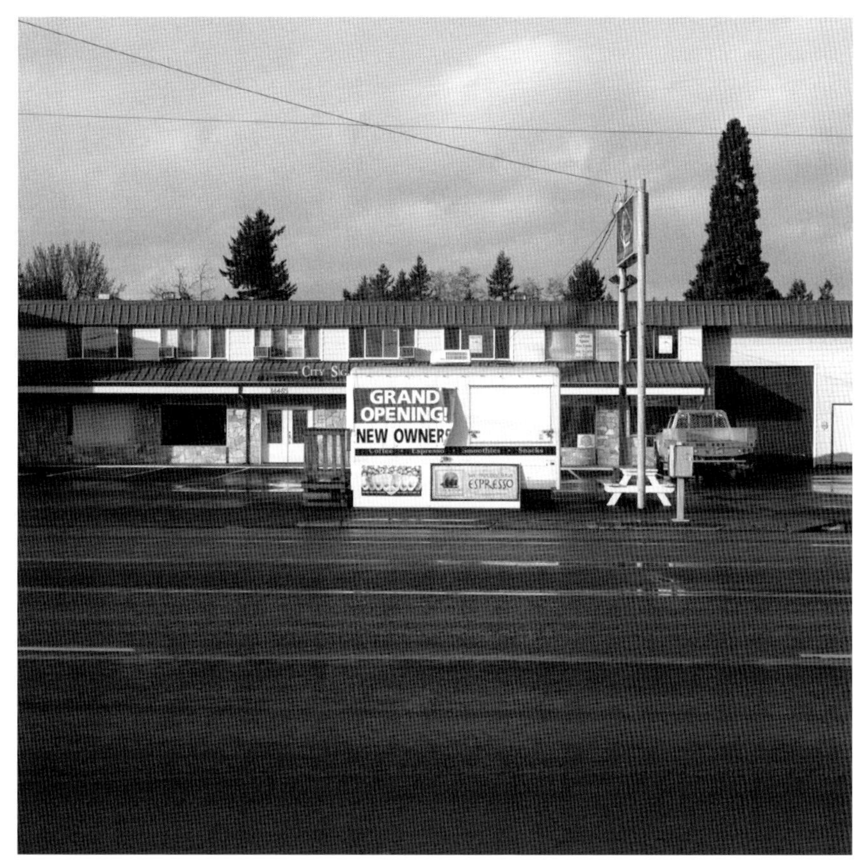

▲ *Sleepy Bear, Portland, Oregon*

◂ *Cascade Coffees, Meridian, Washington*

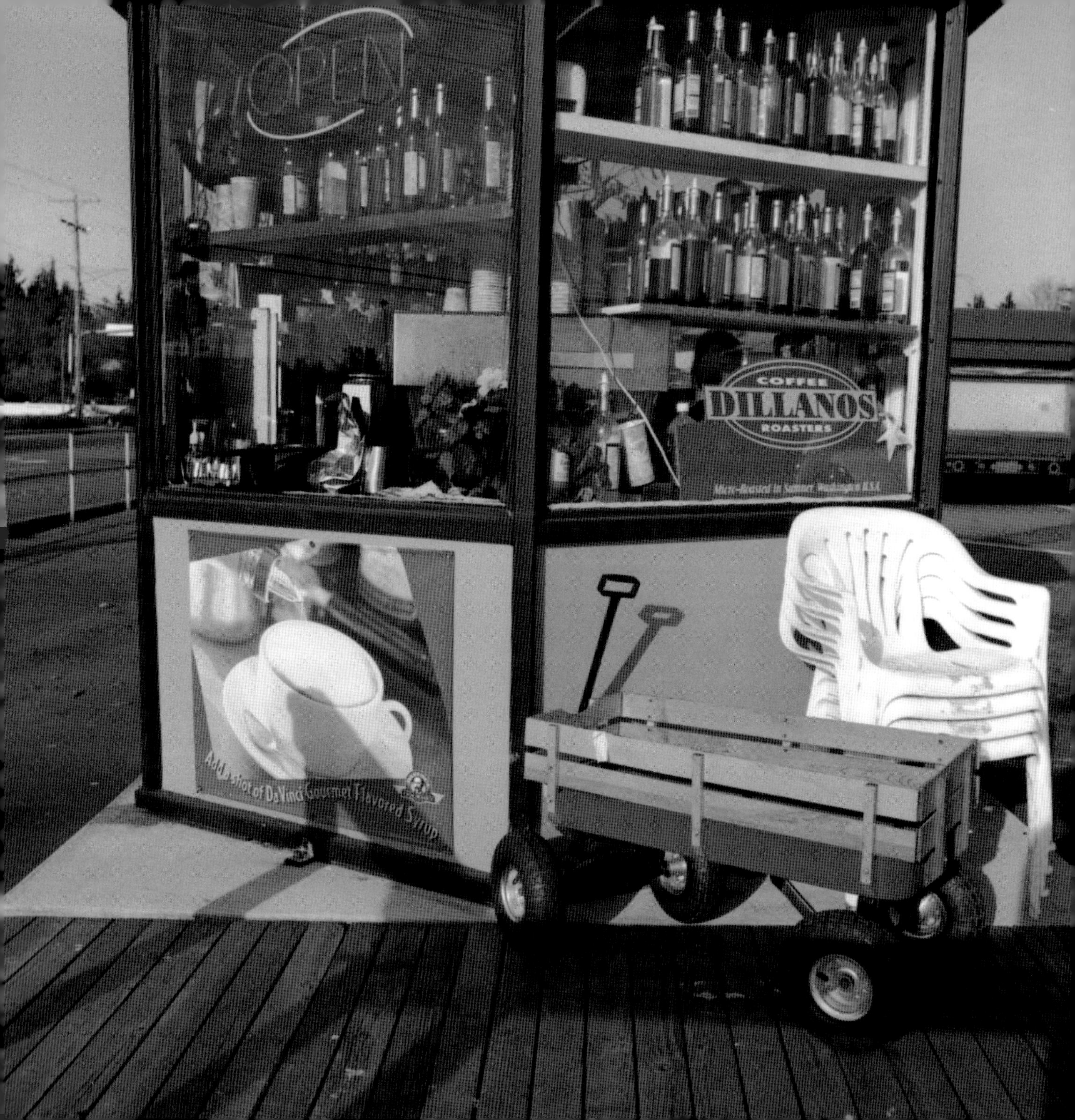
OPEN
COFFEE
DILLANOS
ROASTERS
Add a shot of DaVinci Gourmet Flavored Syrup

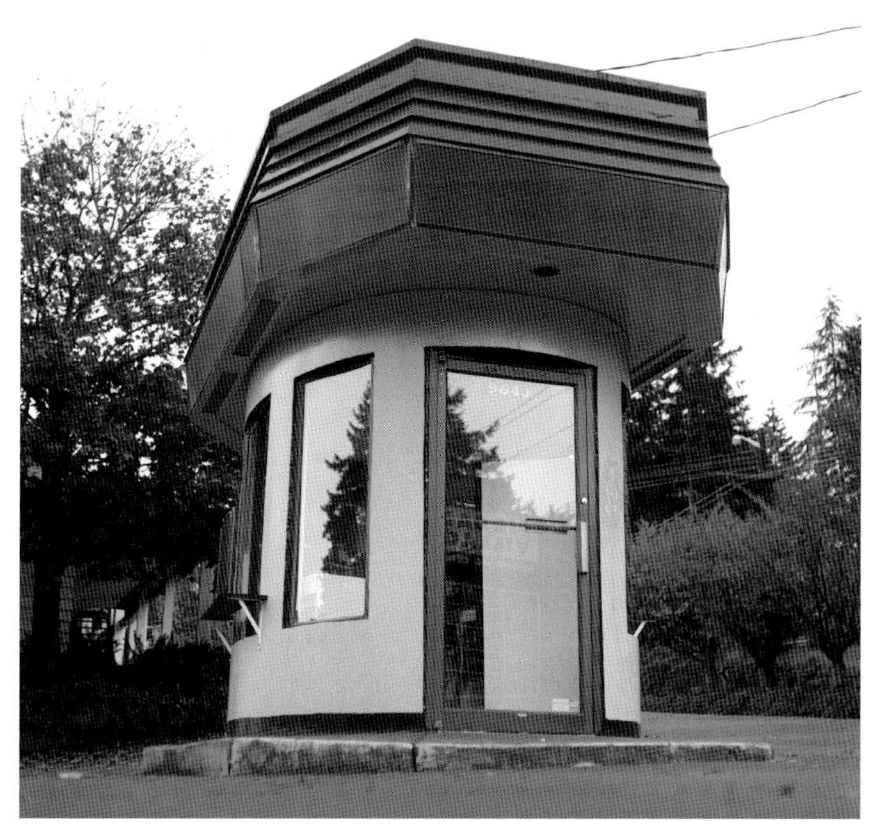

▲ *Unoccupied conversion of a Seattle FilmWorks kiosk, Edmonds, Washington*

◂ *Angel's Espresso, Lynnwood, Washington*

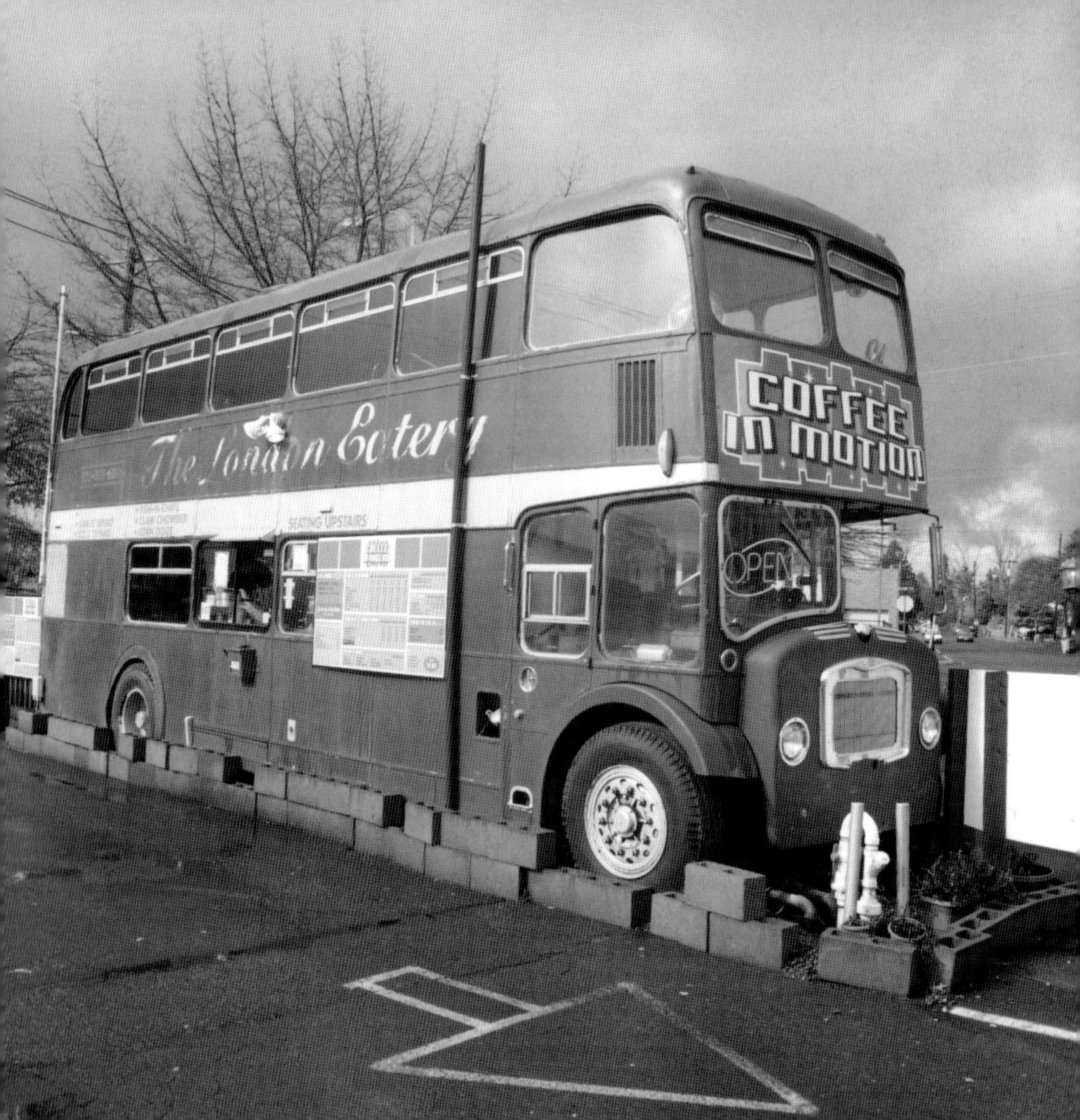
The London Eatery
COFFEE IN MOTION
SEATING UPSTAIRS
OPEN

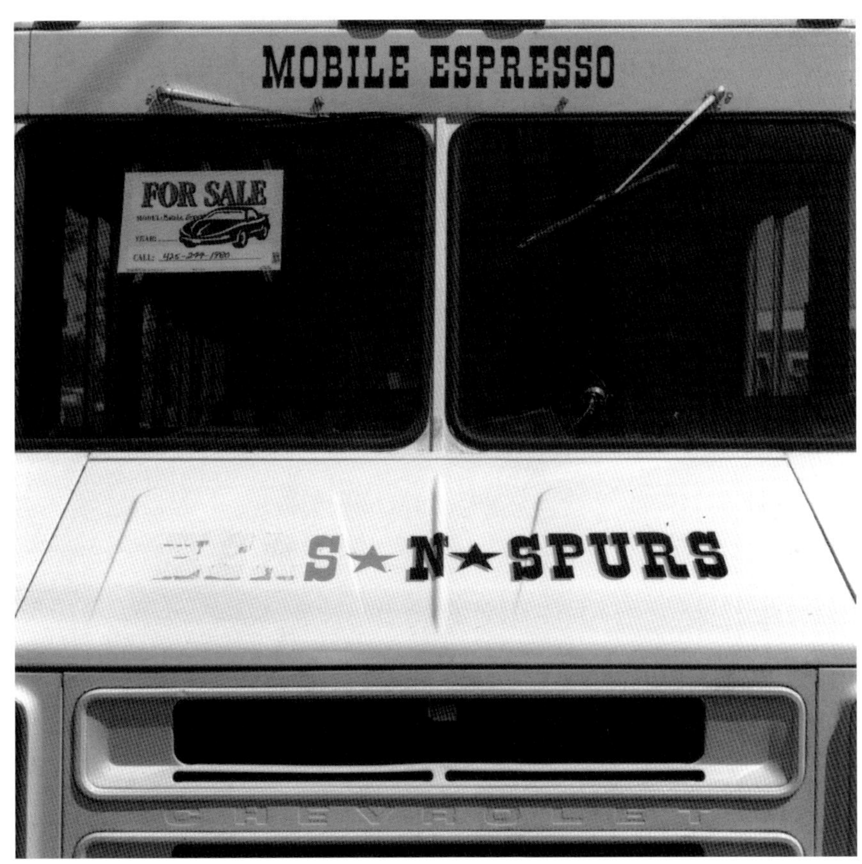

▲ *Hers N Spurs Mobile Espresso, Marysville, Washington*

◂ *Coffee in Motion, Salem, Oregon*

D&M Coffee Co., Winegars, and Pioneer Coffee Co., Ellensburg, Washington

I photographed this former gas station three times, and each time found it had a different owner. As I was finishing work on this book, I found the location unoccupied.

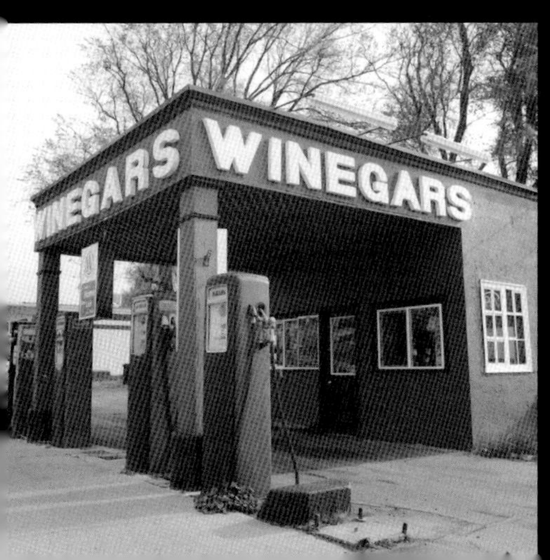

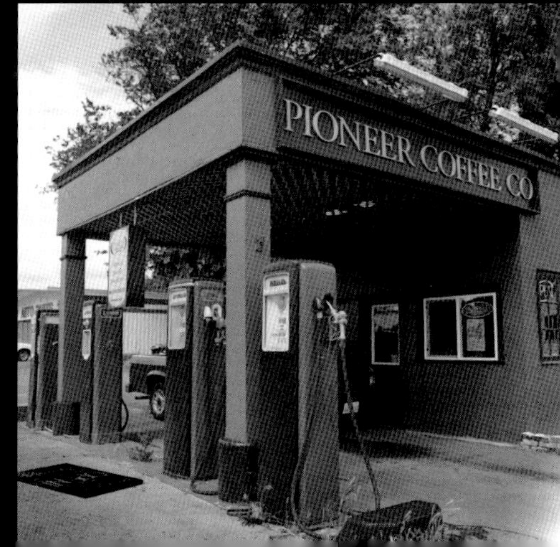

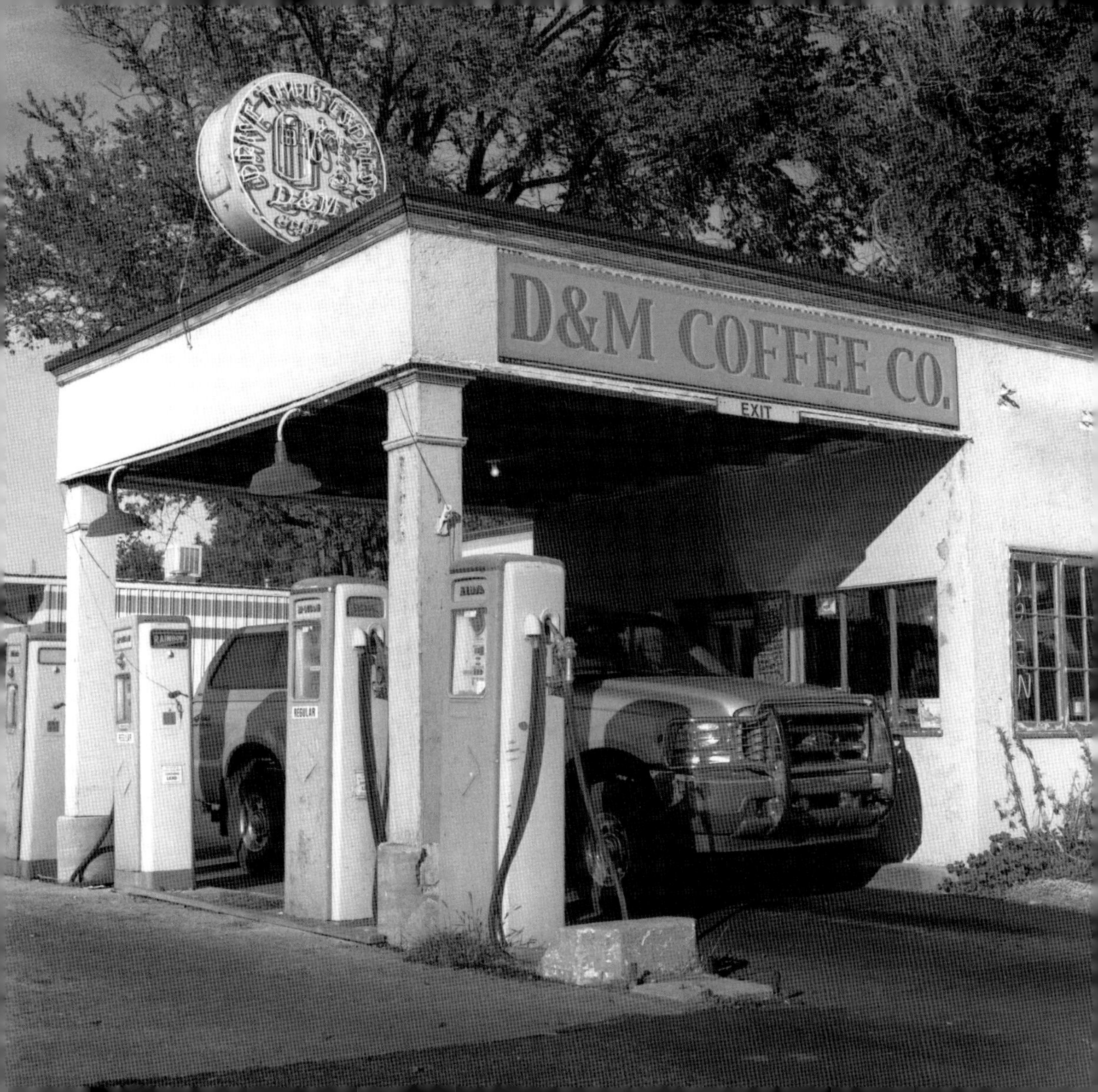
D&M COFFEE CO.
EXIT
RAINBOW
REGULAR

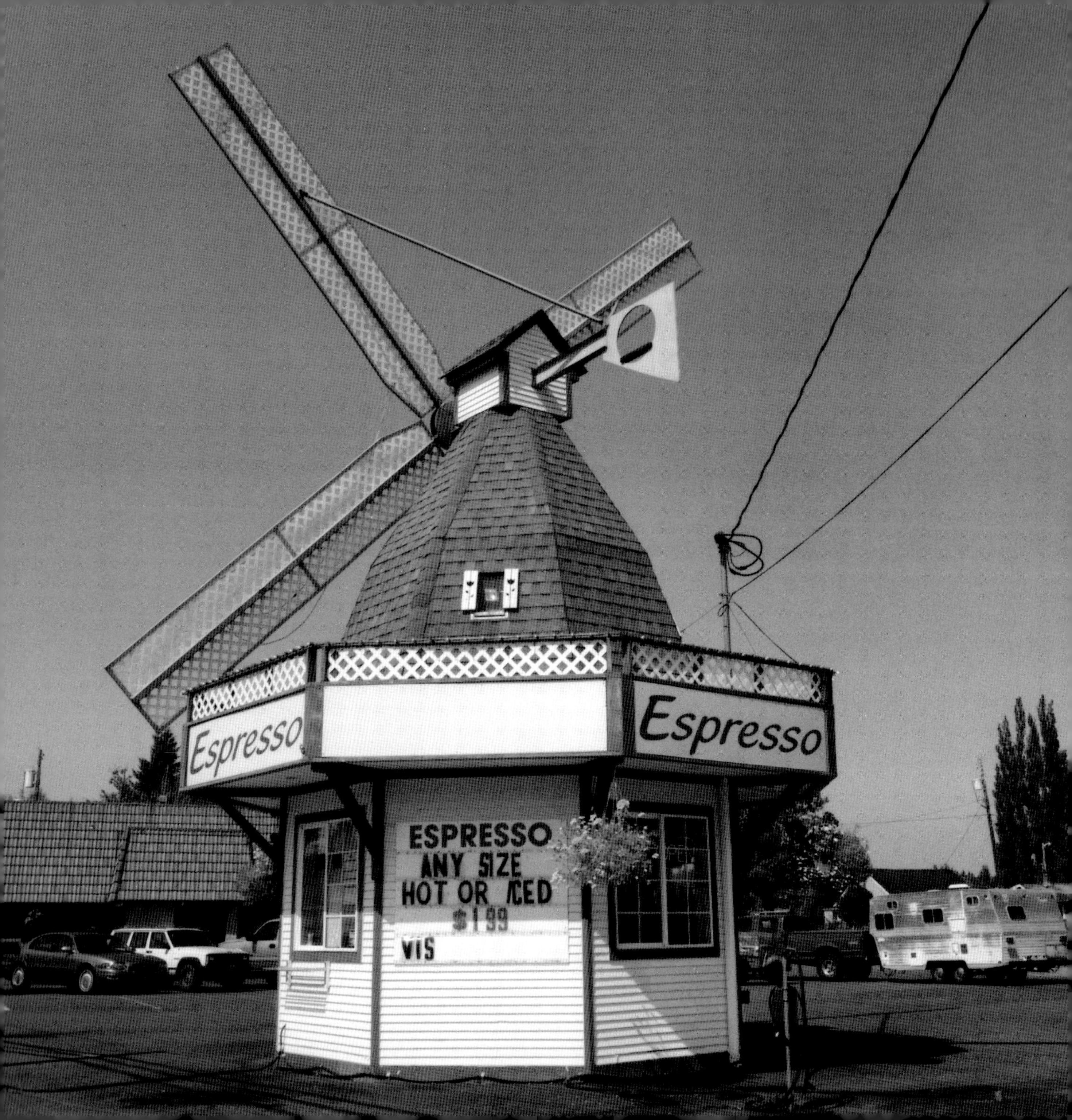

Espresso
Espresso
ESPRESSO
ANY SIZE
HOT OR ICED
$1.99
VIS

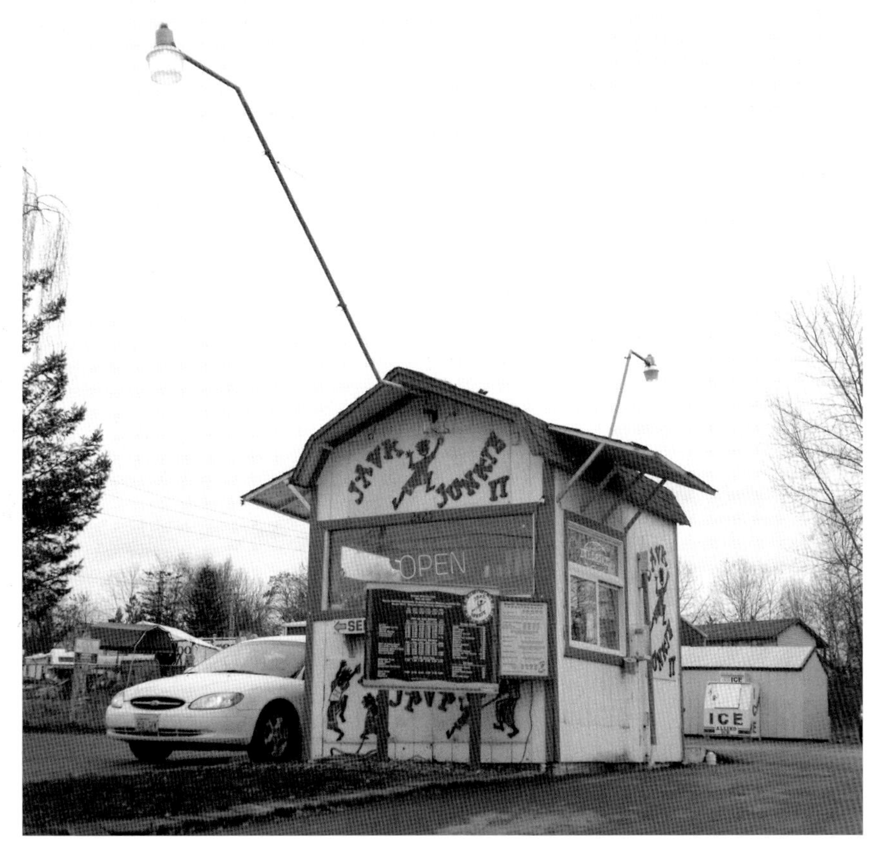

▲ *Java Junkie II, Edgewood, Washington*

◀ *The Windmill, Sultan, Washington*

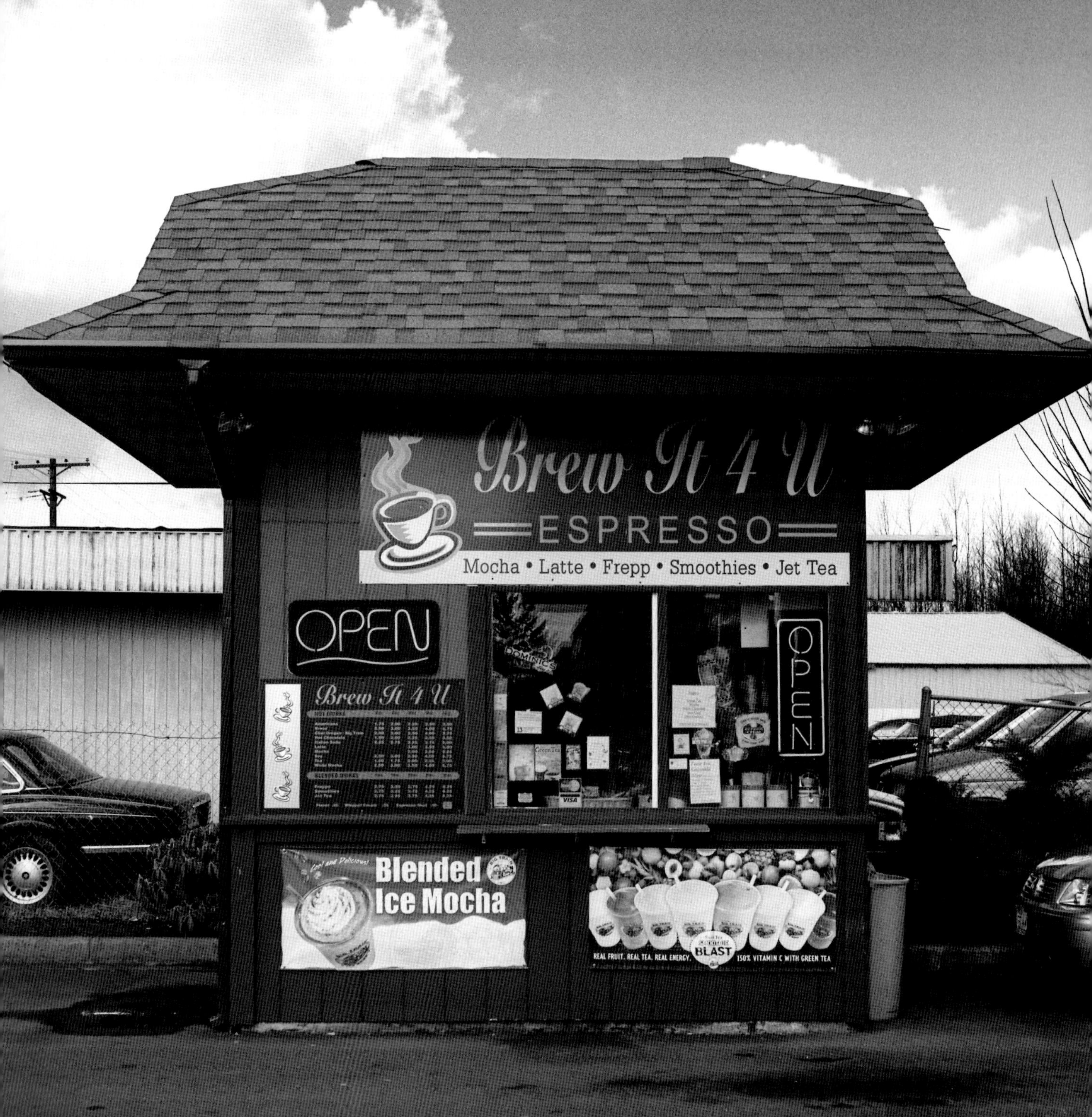
Brew It 4 U
ESPRESSO
Mocha • Latte • Frepp • Smoothies • Jet Tea
OPEN
Brew It 4 U
OPEN
Blended
Ice Mocha
REAL FRUIT. REAL TEA. REAL ENERGY.
BLAST
150% VITAMIN C WITH GREEN TEA

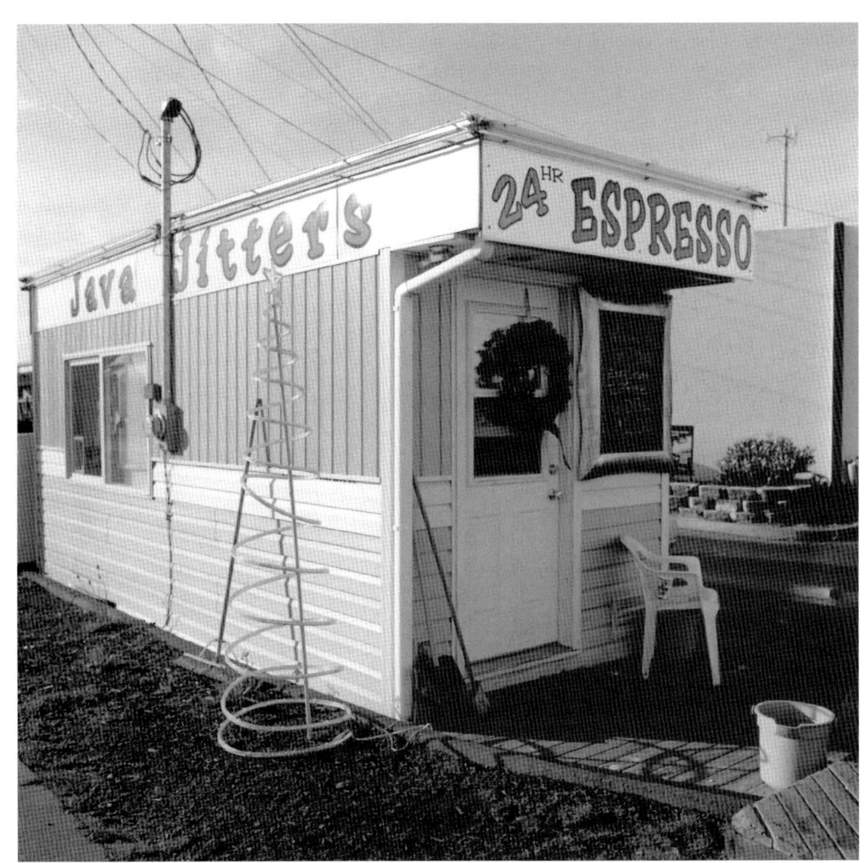

▲ *Java Jitters, Lynnwood, Washington*

◂ *Brew It 4 U, Tacoma, Washington*

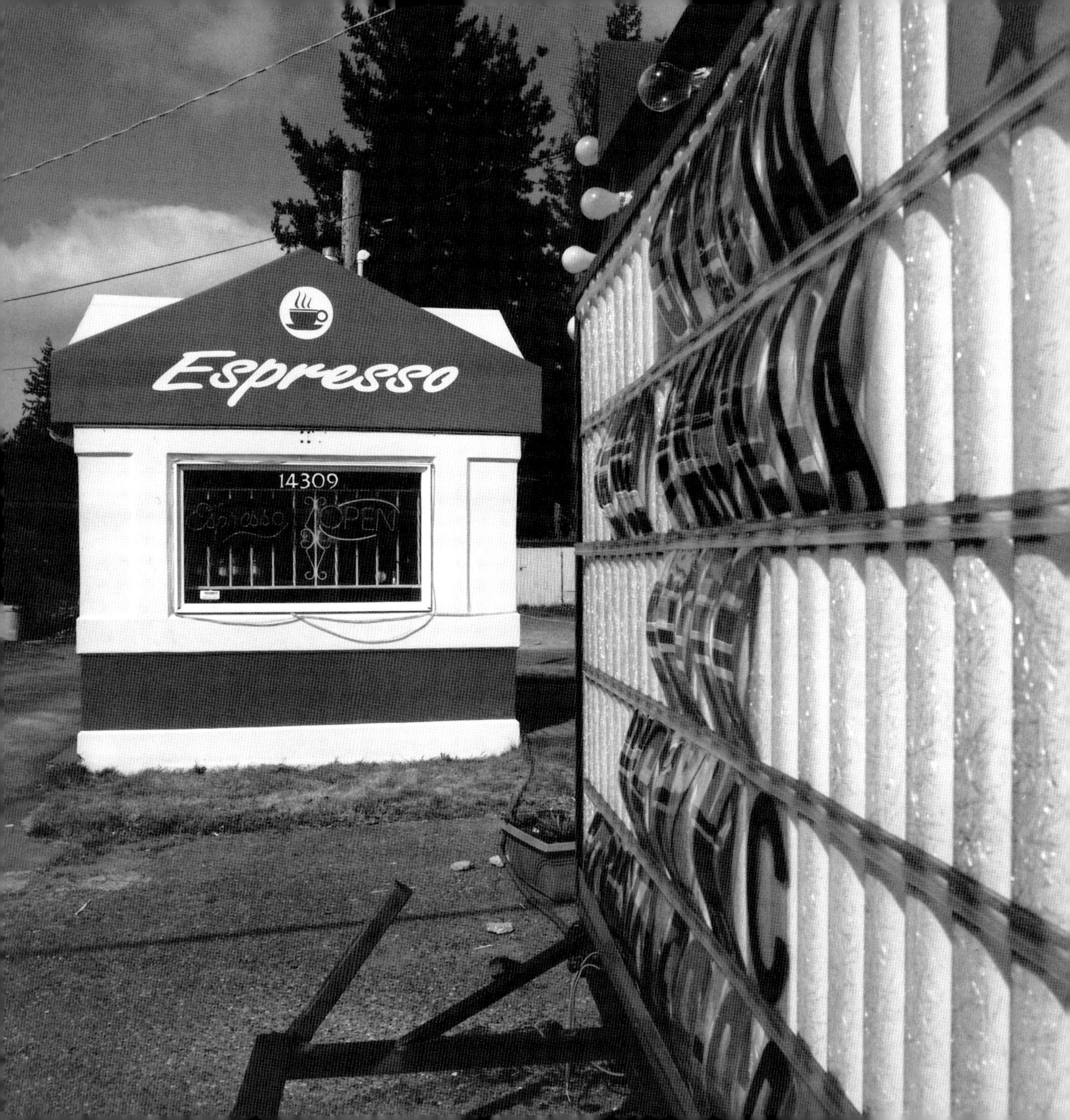
Espresso
14309
Espresso
OPEN

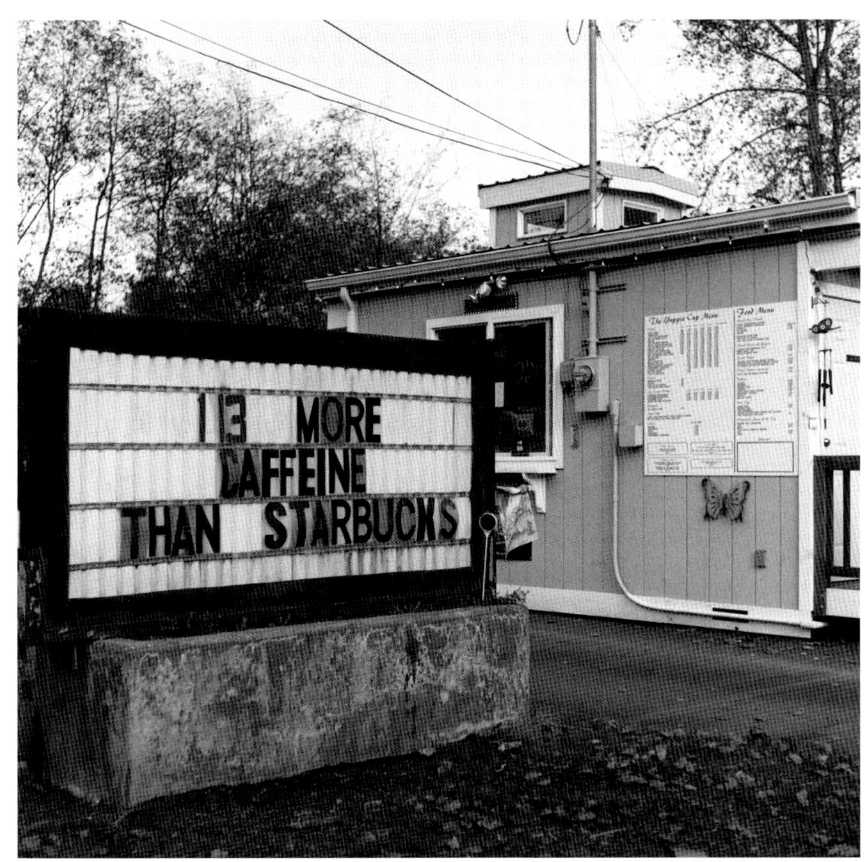

▲ *The Yuppie Cup, Bothell, Washington*

◀ *Greenwood Grind, Seattle, Washington*

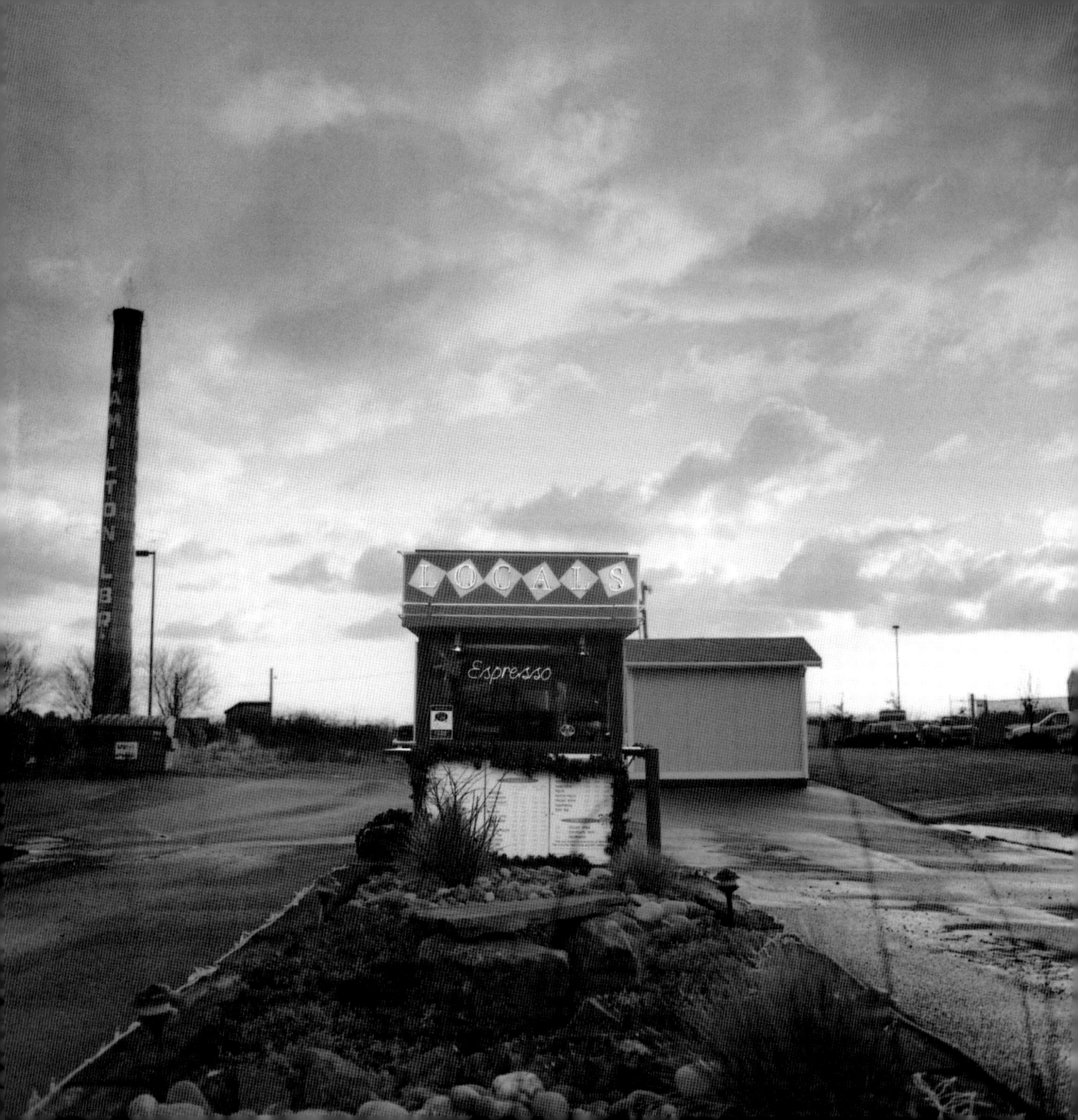
HAMILTON LBR.
LOCALS
Espresso

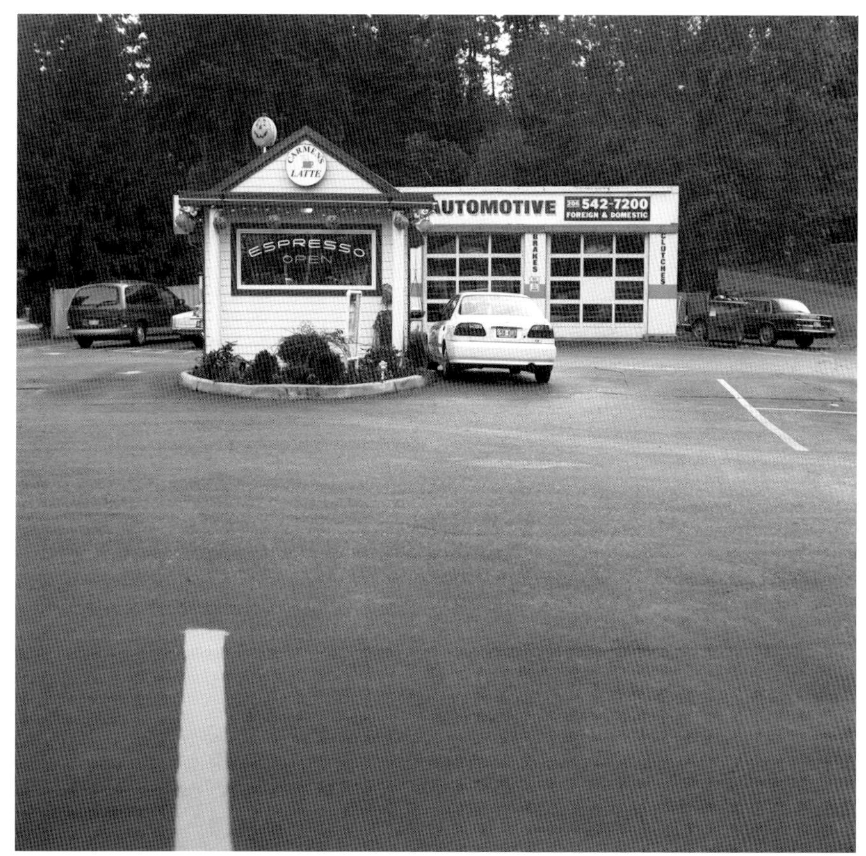

▲ *Carmen's Latte, Edmonds, Washington*

◀ *Locals, Stanwood, Washington*

Rocket Express and Pik-me-up Espresso,

Bellingham, Washington

These two photos are of the same building but with different owners and very different styles. The building itself, originally a filling station, is the oldest surviving structure on this Bellingham commercial strip.

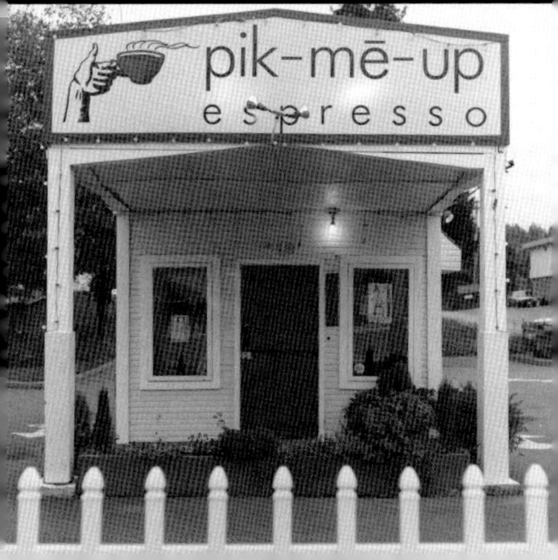

ROCKET EXPRESS
DONUTS & ESPRESSO

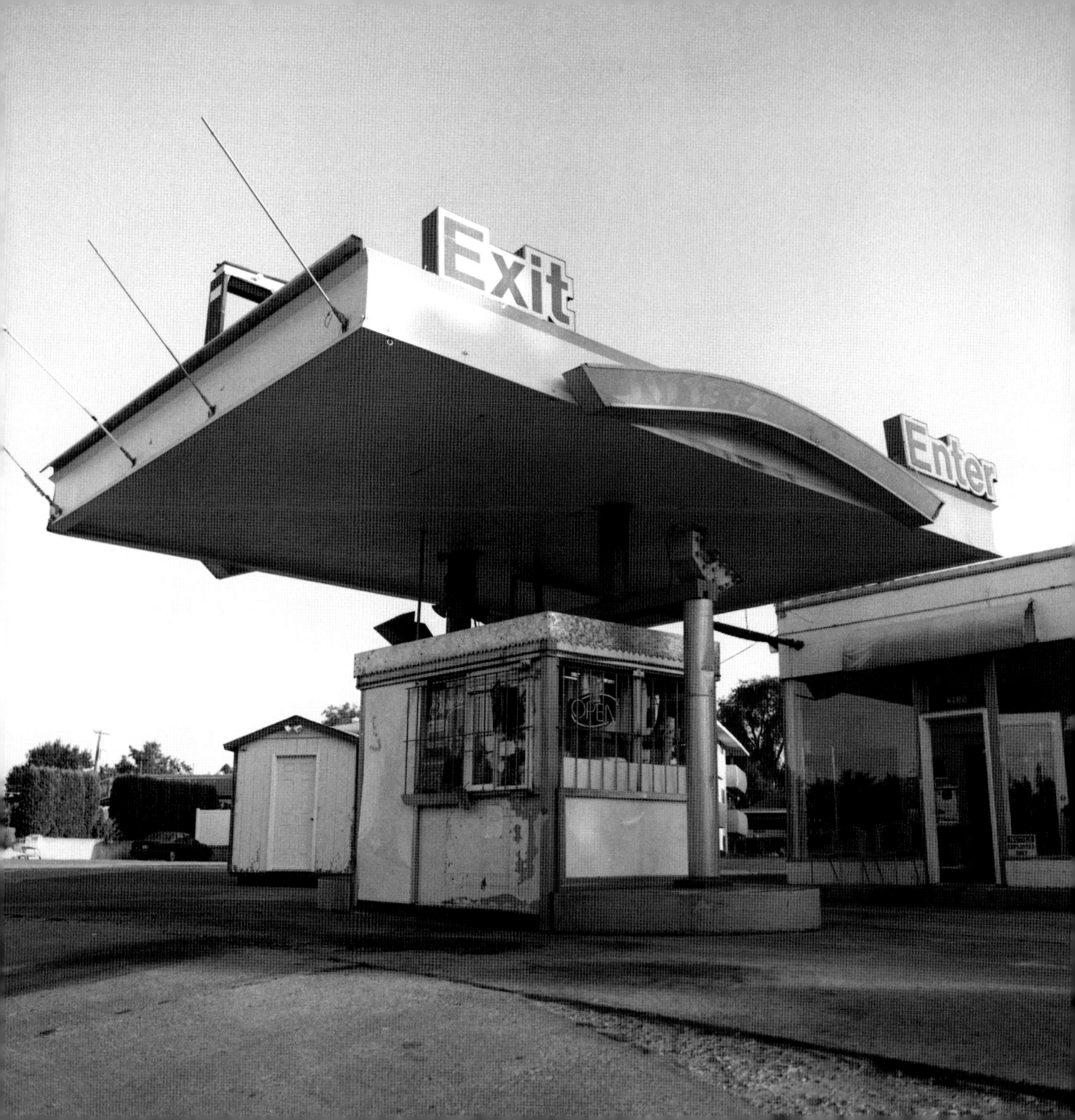
Exit
Enter
OPEN

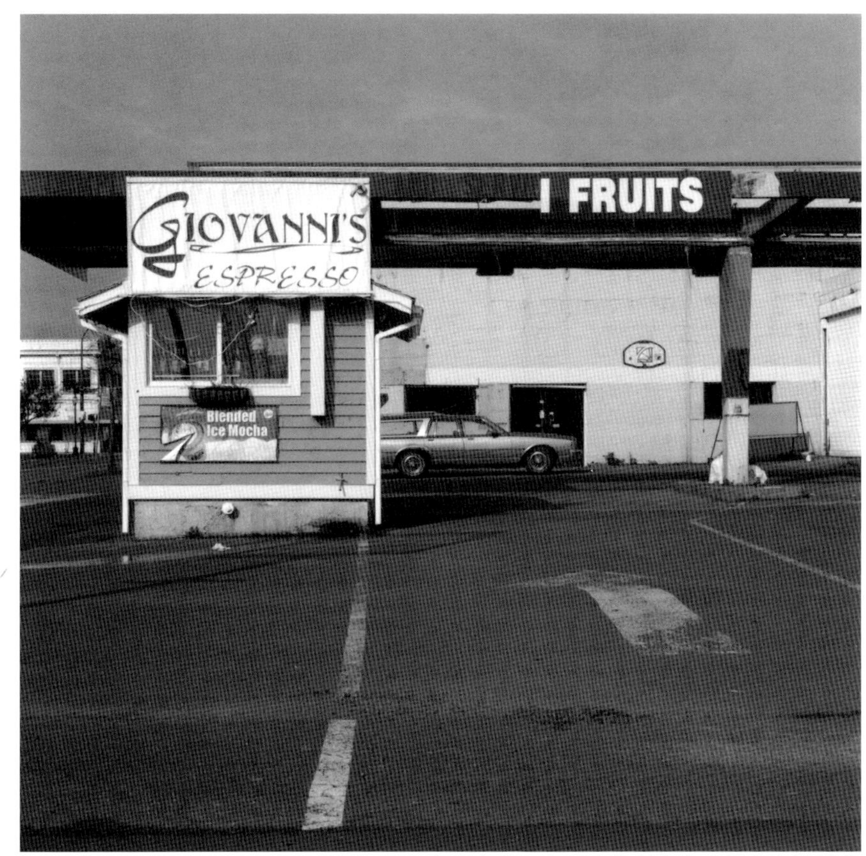

▲ *Giovanni's Espresso, Aberdeen, Washington*

◂ *Jitterz Java, Spokane, Washington*

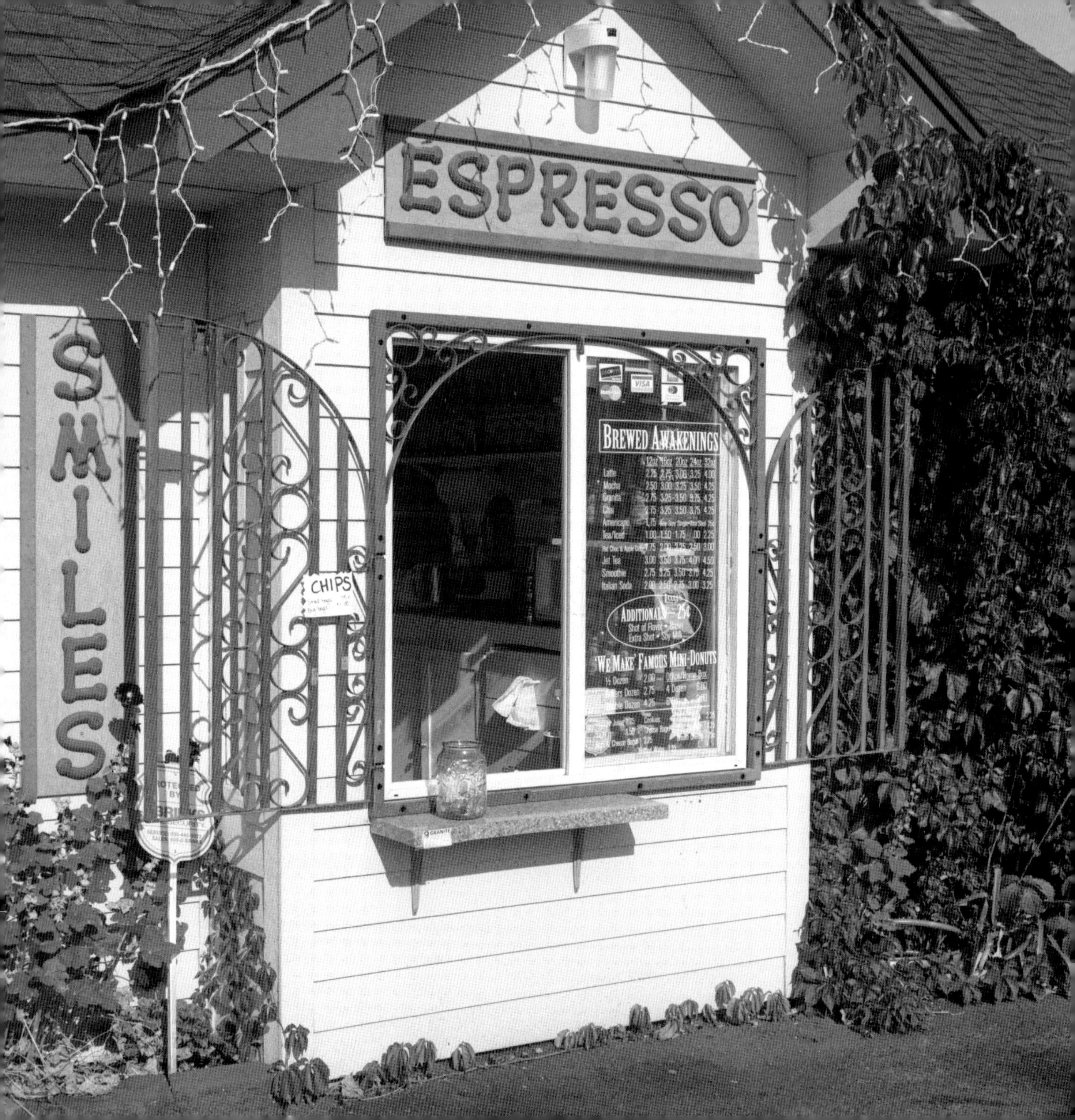
ESPRESSO
SMILES
CHIPS
VISA
BREWED AWAKENINGS
12oz 16oz 20oz 24oz 32oz
Latte
Mocha 2.50 3.00 3.25 3.50 4.25
Granita
Chai 2.75 3.25 3.50 3.75 4.25
Americano 1.75
Tea/Iced
Jet Tea 3.00 3.50 3.75 4.00 4.50
Smoothie
Italian Soda
ADDITIONALS — 25¢
'WE MAKE' FAMOUS MINI-DONUTS
½ Dozen 2.00
4 Dozen 6.00

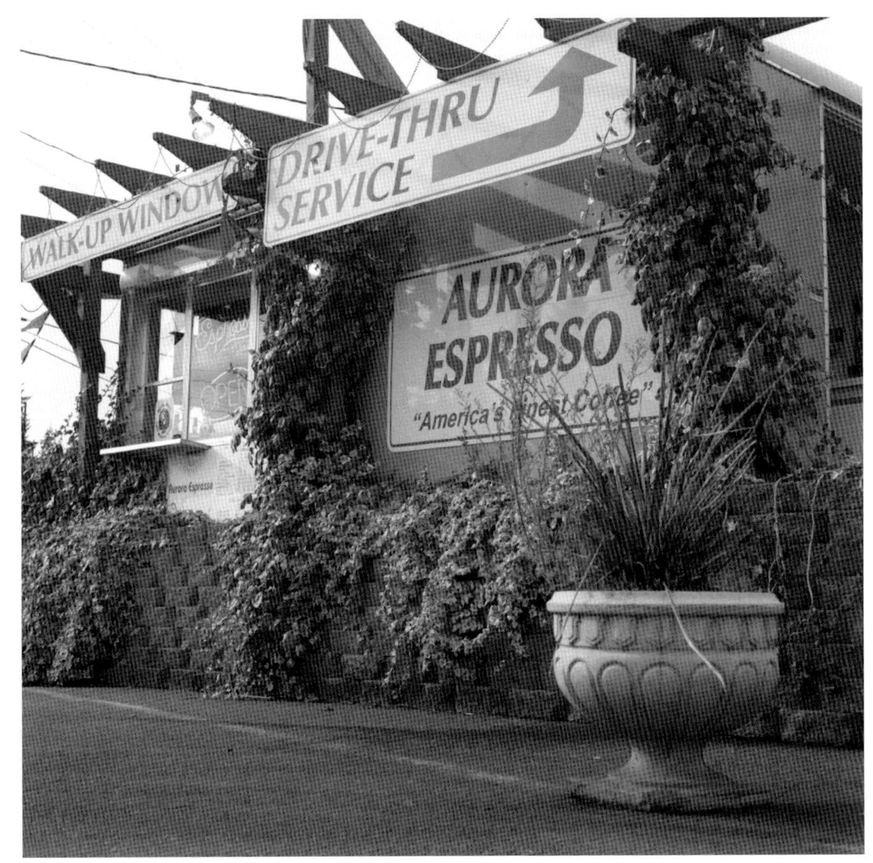

▲ *Aurora Espresso, Shoreline, Washington*

◀ *Brewed Awakenings, Spokane, Washington*

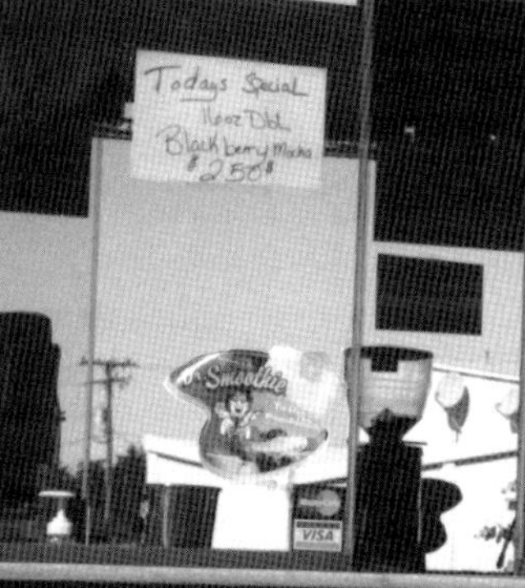
Todays Special
Blackberry Mocha
$2.50

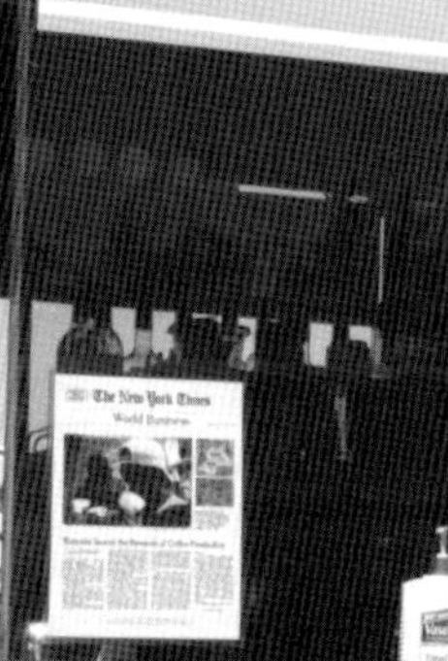

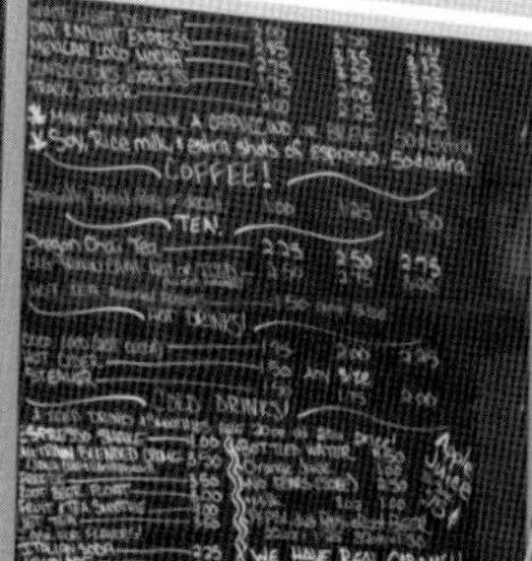
The New York Times

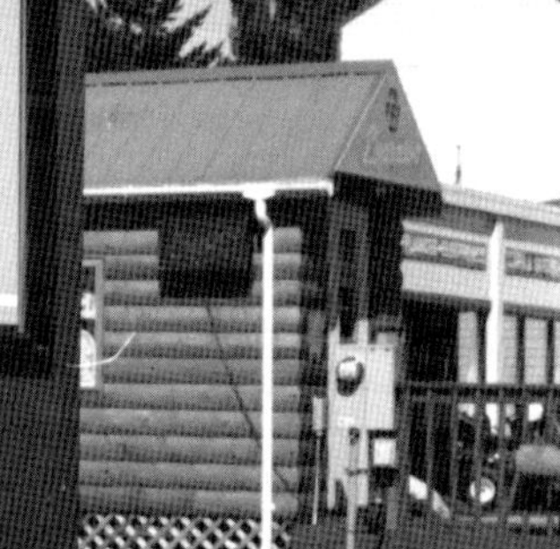
BAGELS
SHAKES
ESPRESS-O
BISCUITS & GRAVY
THE MARKET BIN
Express-O

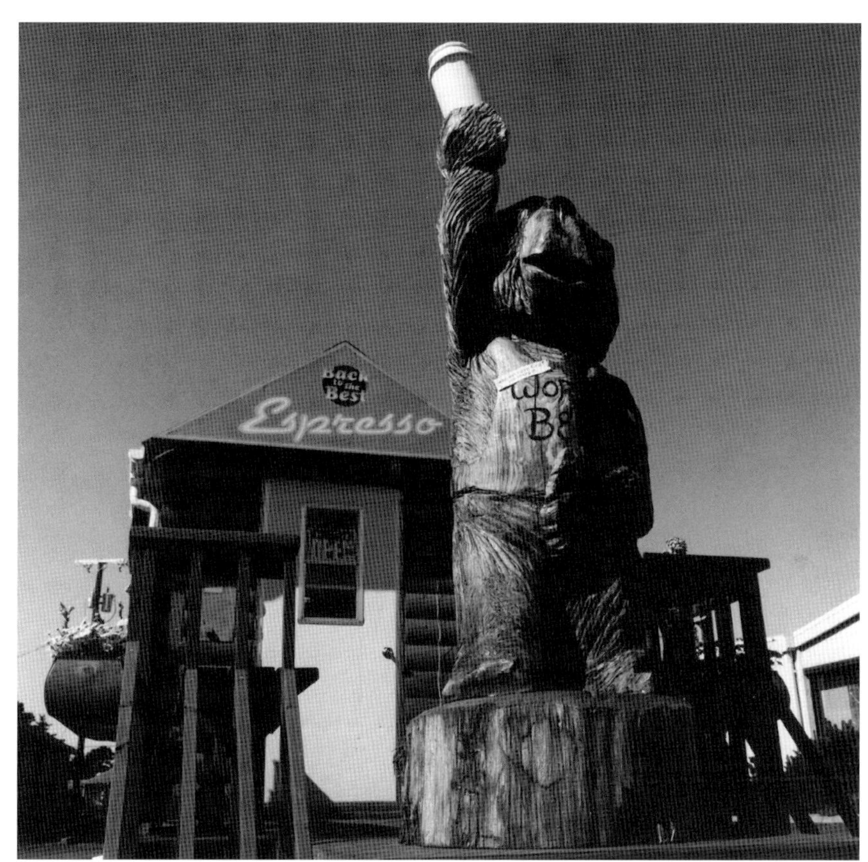

▲ *Back to the Best Espresso, Florence, Oregon*

◀ *The Market Bin Express-O, Florence, Oregon*

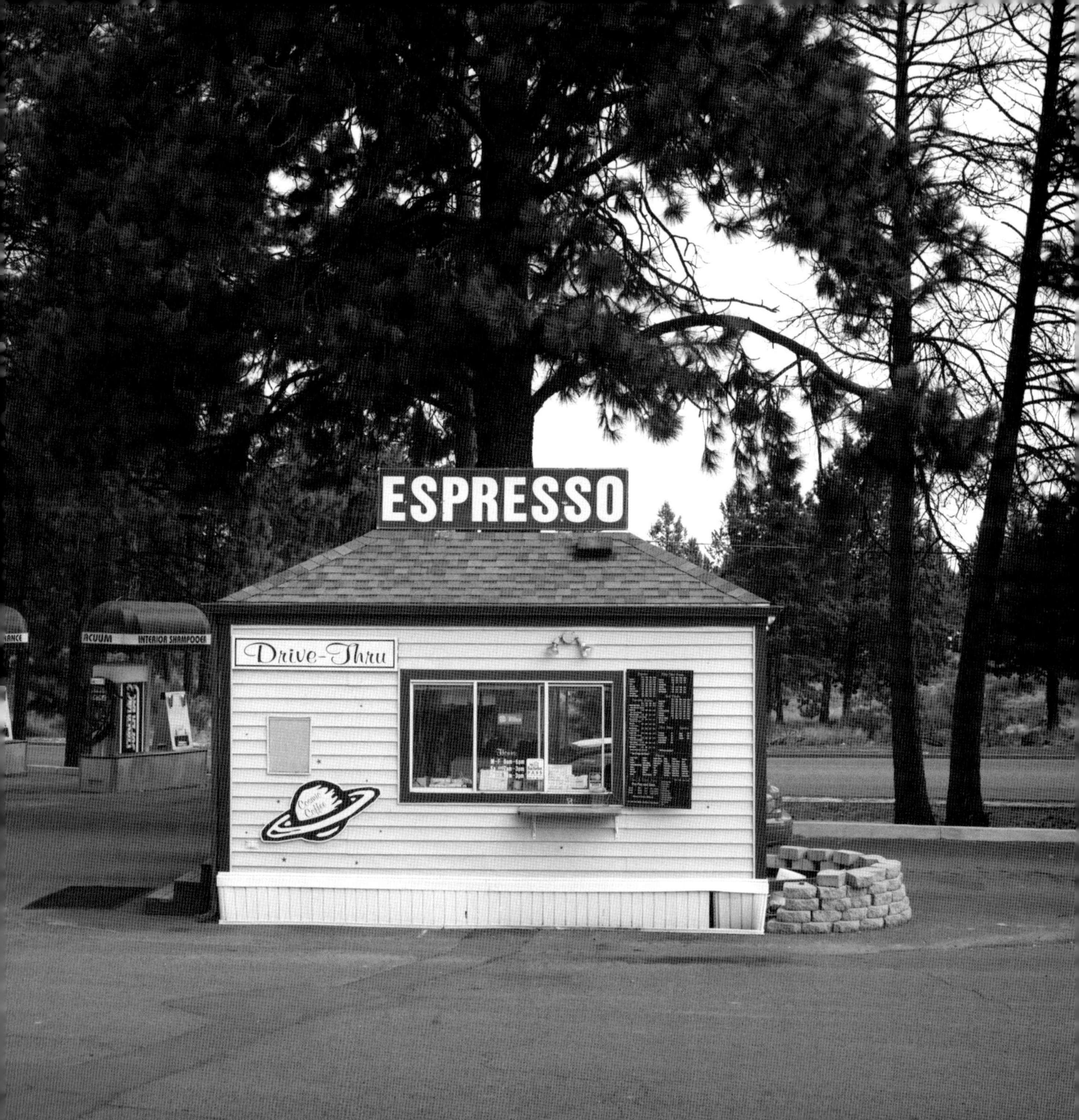
ESPRESSO
Drive-Thru
INTERIOR SHAMPOOER
Cosmic Coffee

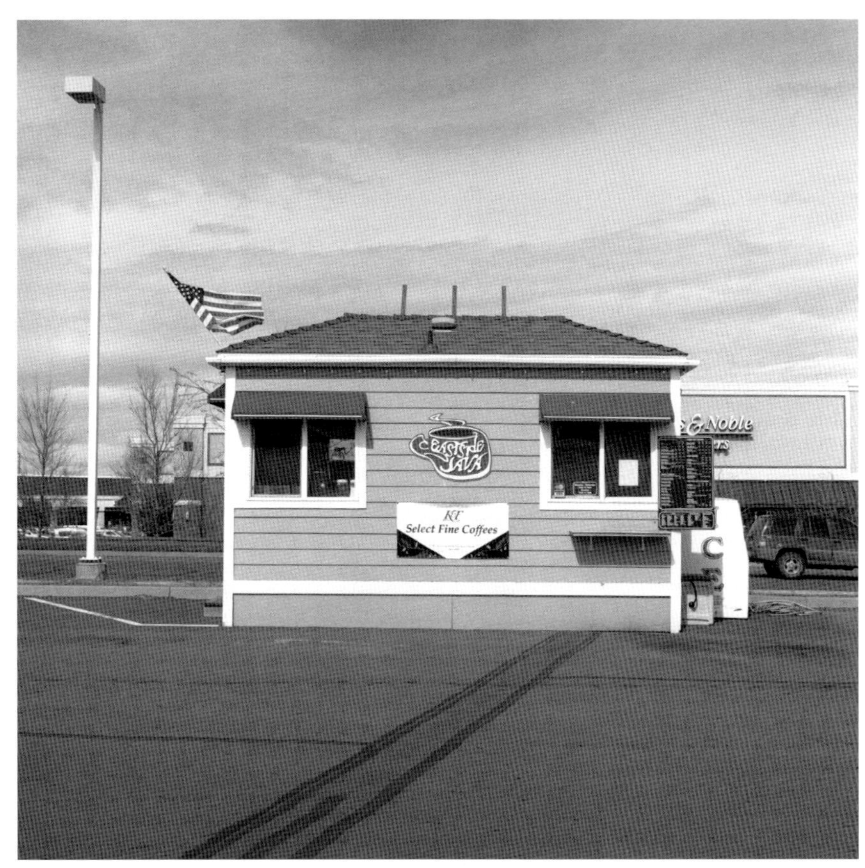

▲ *Eastside Java, Bend, Oregon*

◂ *Cosmic Coffee, Bend, Oregon*

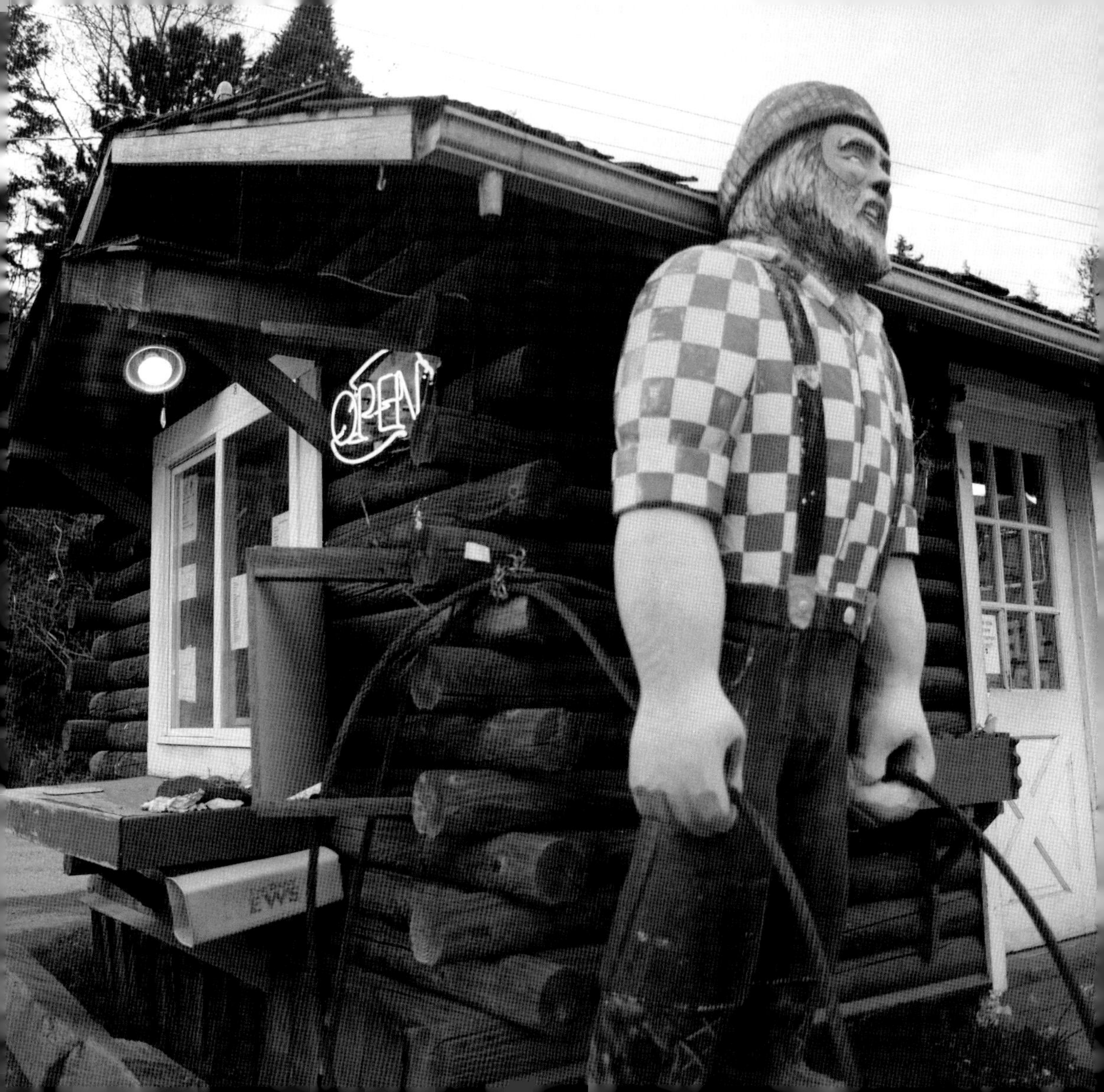
OPEN

Log Cabin Espresso, *Discovery Bay, Washington.*

This building was constructed of peeler cords from a local veneer mill, and stood empty for years before being used briefly as a real estate office, and then opening as Log Cabin Espresso in 1992. It is the only espresso stand I know of that sells fresh oysters.

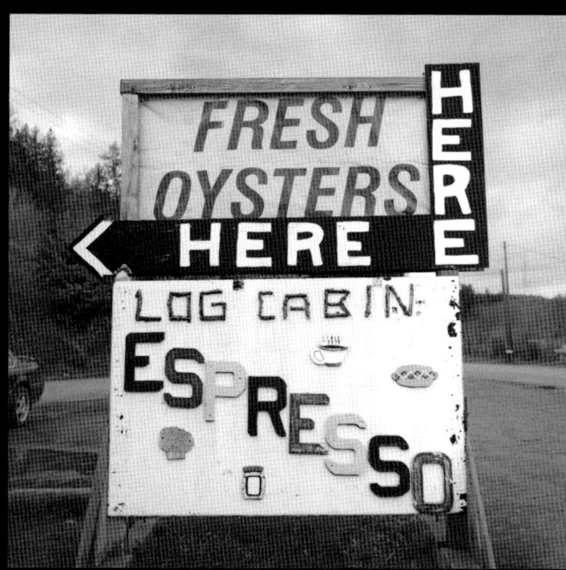

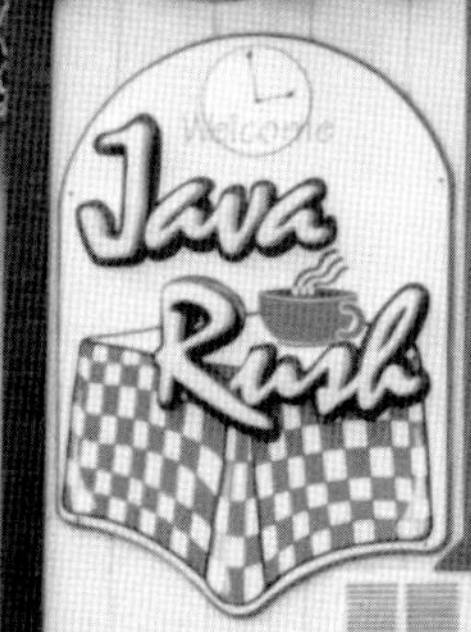
Welcome
Java Rush

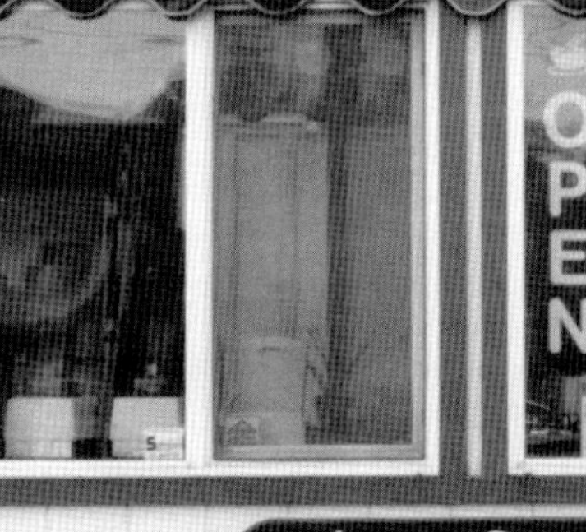

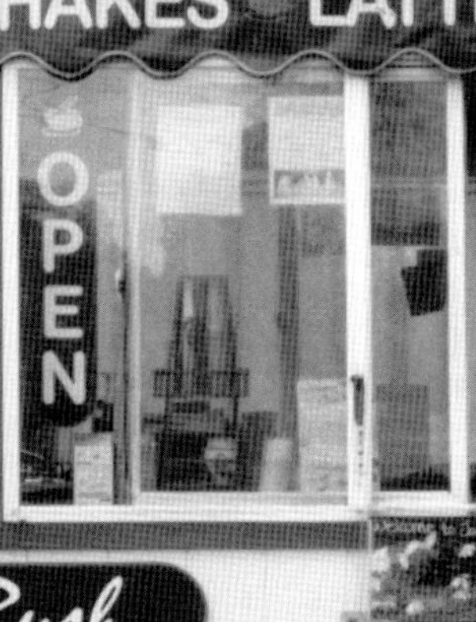
OPEN

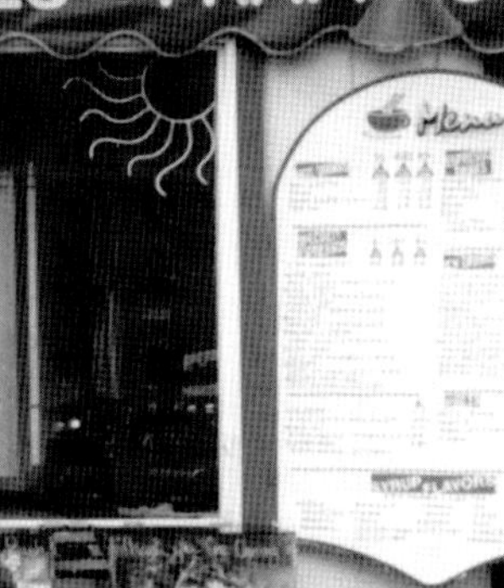
Menu

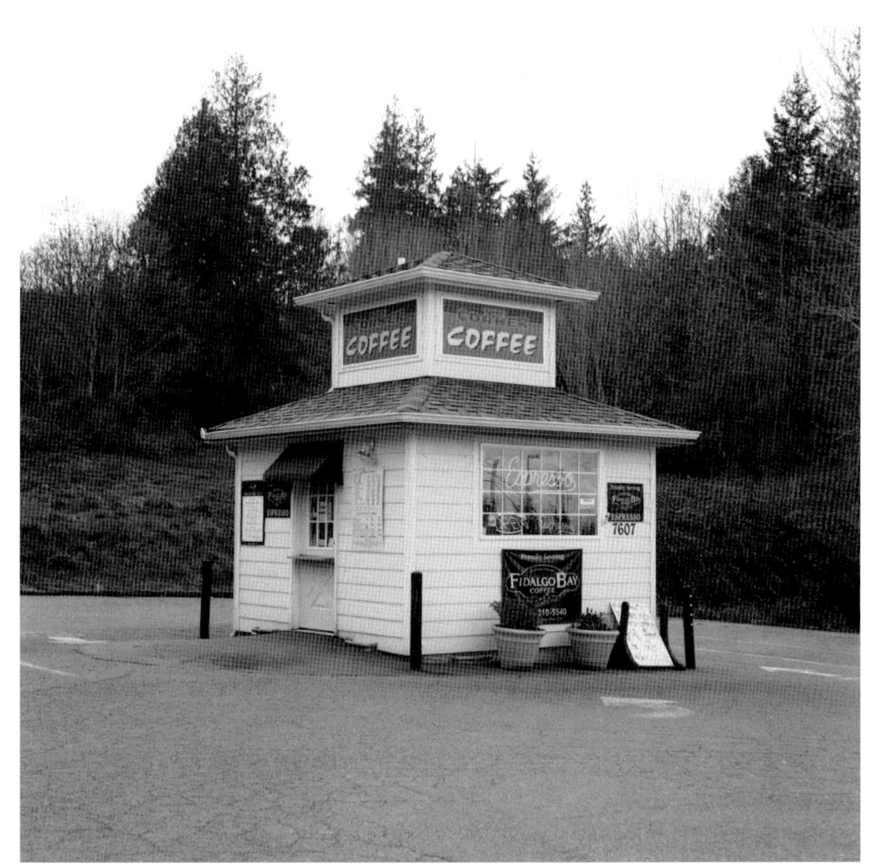

▲ *The Corner Coffee, Anacortes, Washington*

◂ *Java Rush, Bend, Oregon*

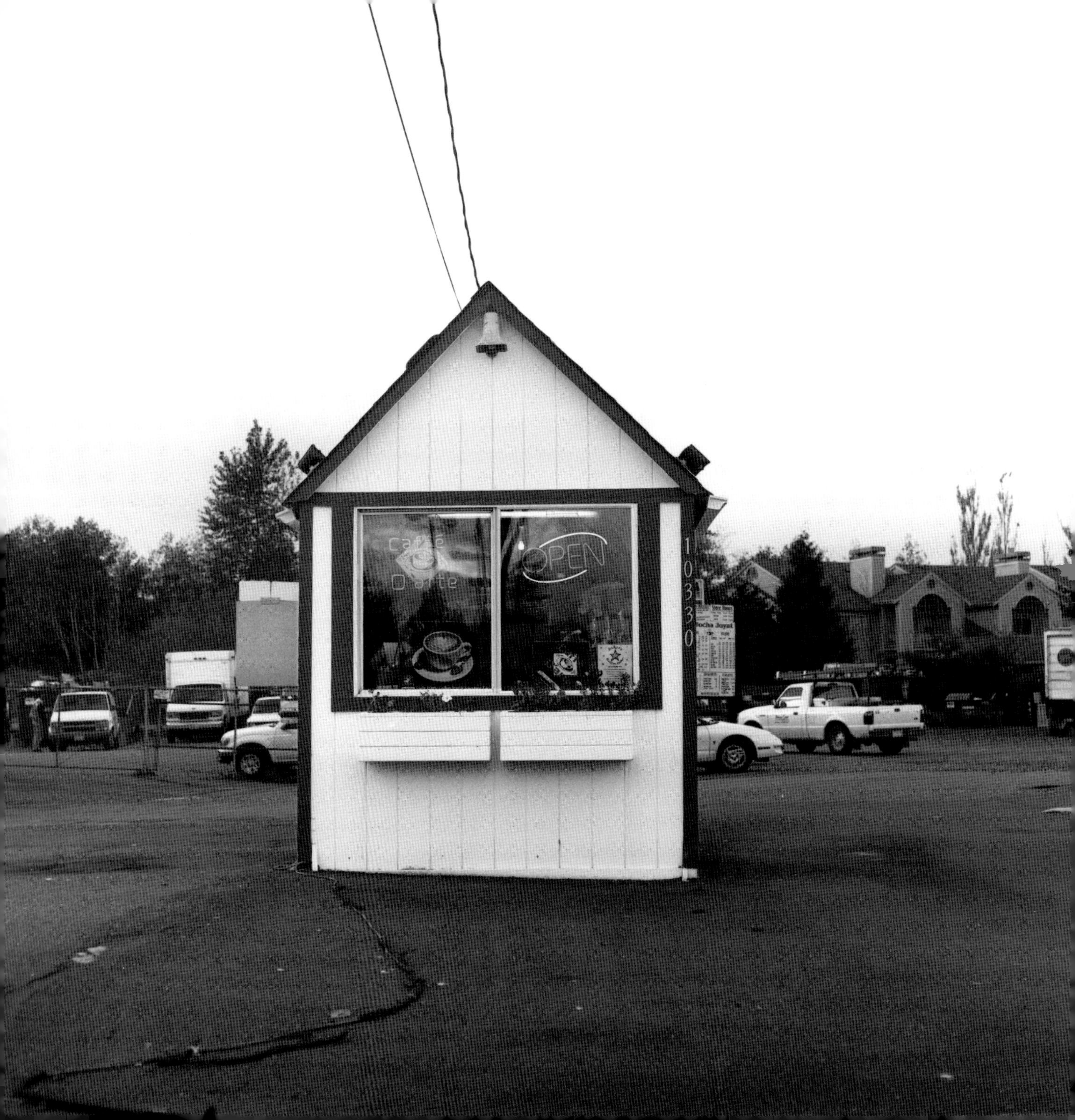
Caffé
D'arte
OPEN
10330

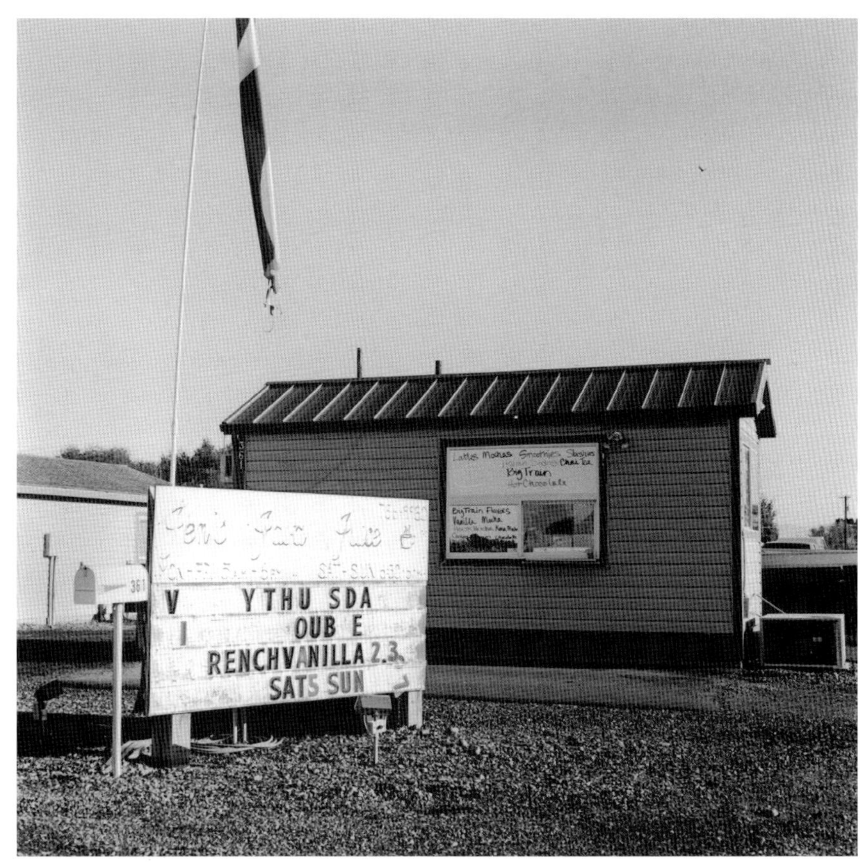

▲ *Jen's Java Juice, Prosser, Washington*

◀ *Mocha Joynt, Everett, Washington*

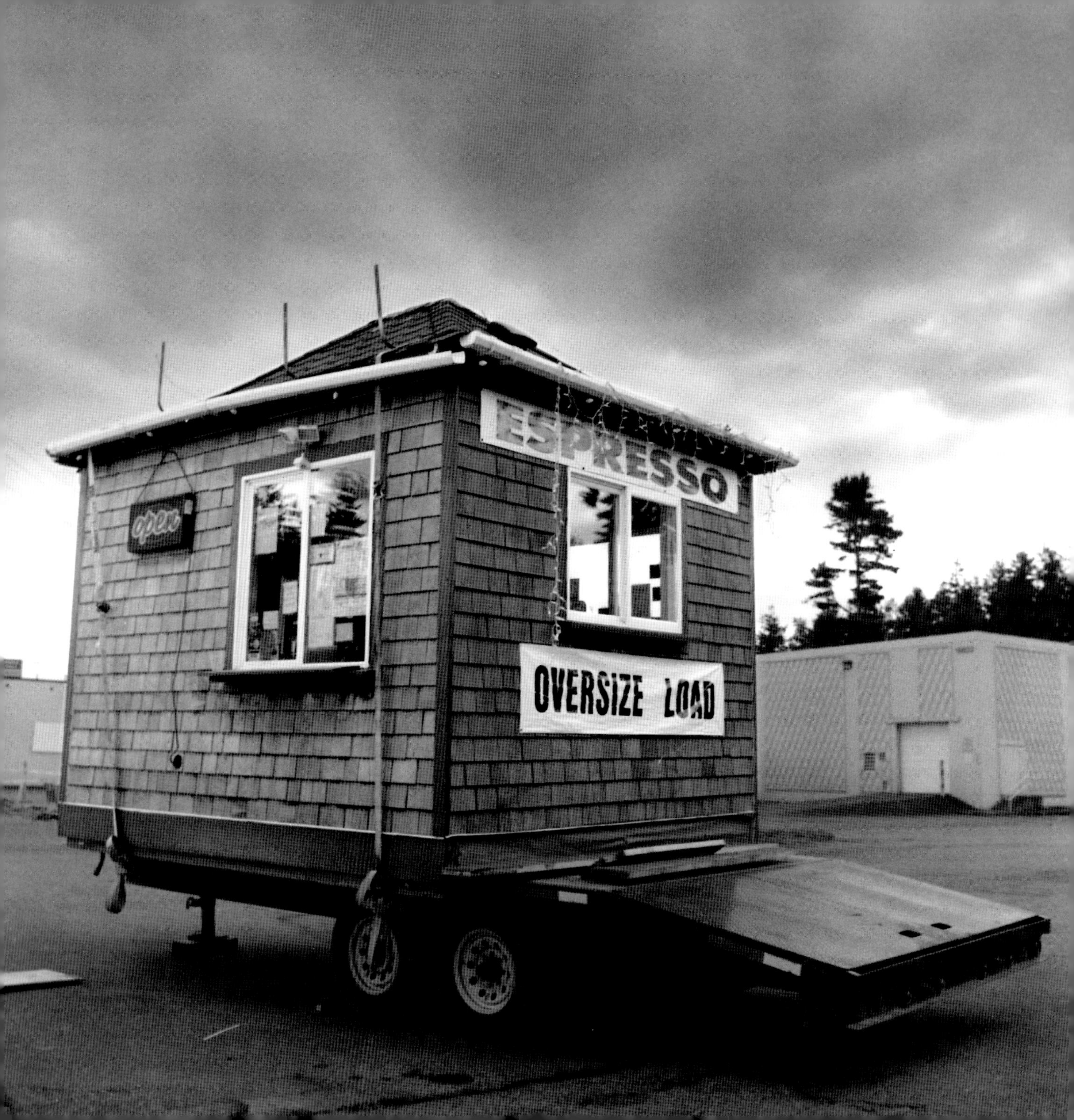
open
ESPRESSO
OVERSIZE LOAD

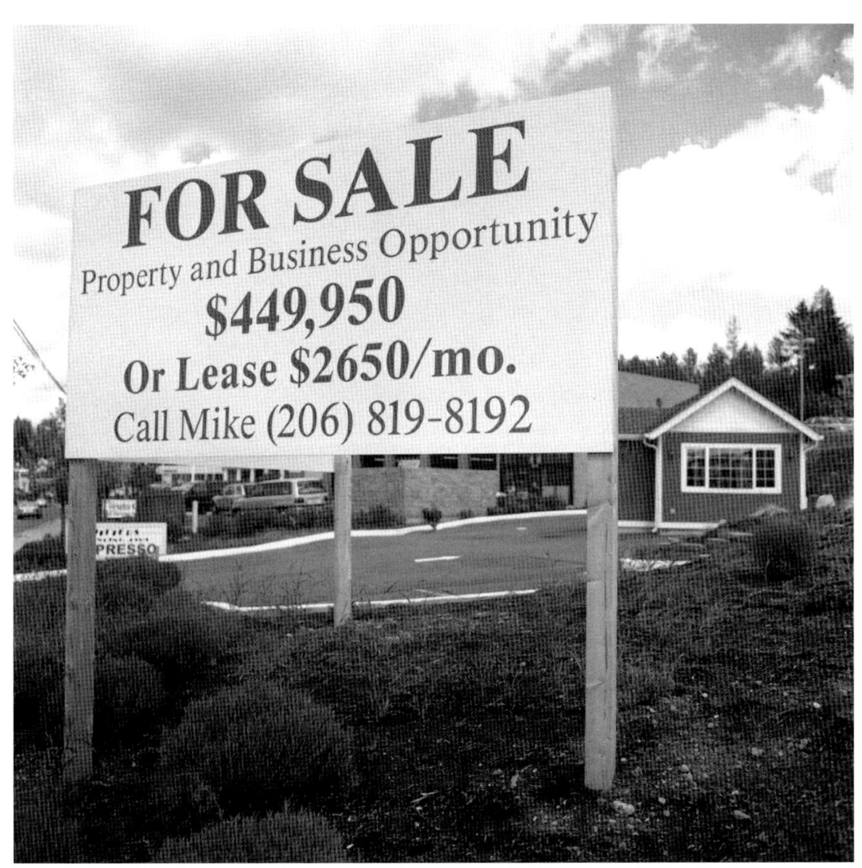

▲ *For sale, Lynnwood, Washington*

◂ *Oversize load, Lynnwood, Washington*

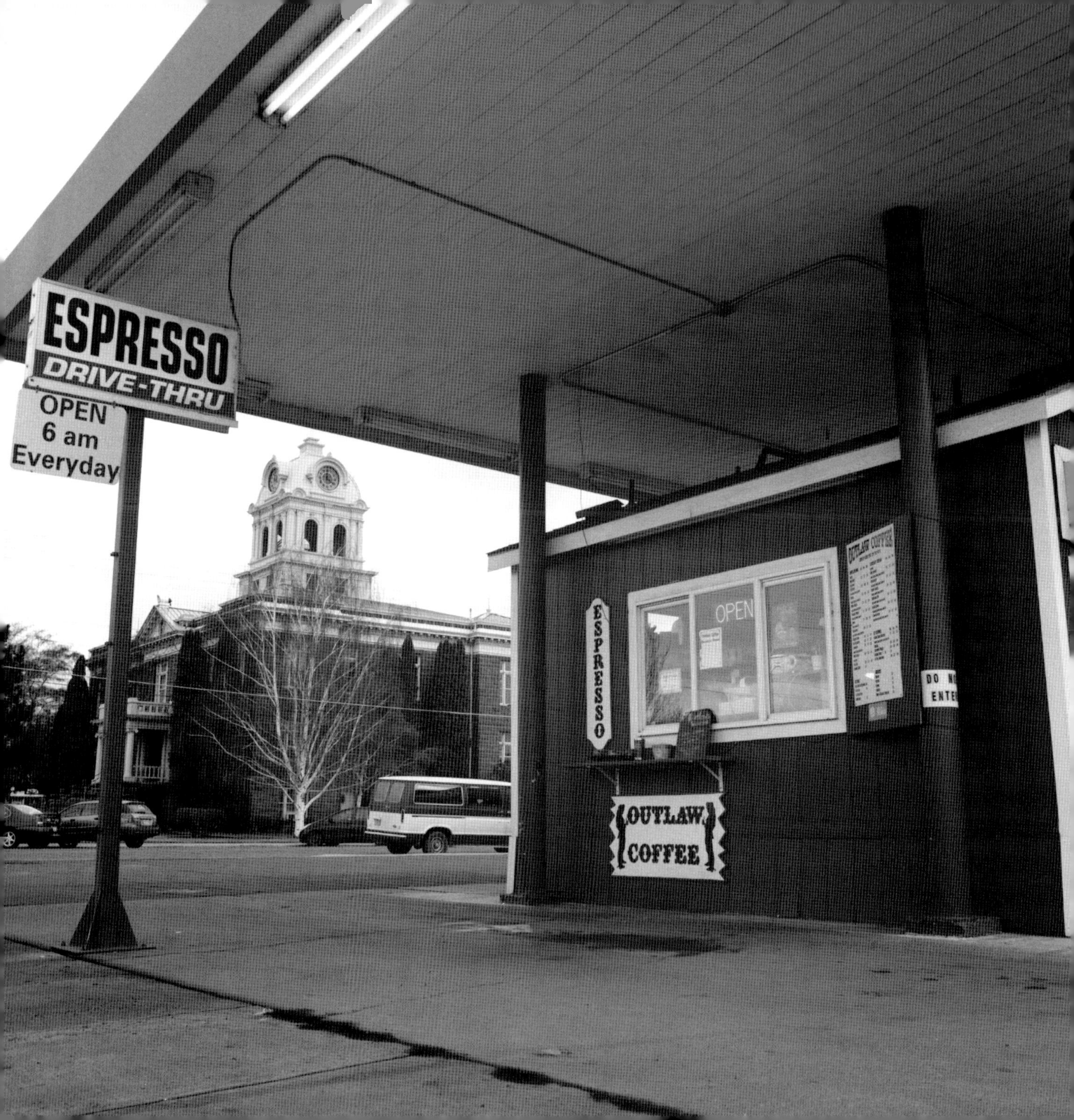
ESPRESSO
DRIVE-THRU
OPEN
6 am
Everyday
ESPRESSO
OPEN
OUTLAW
COFFEE

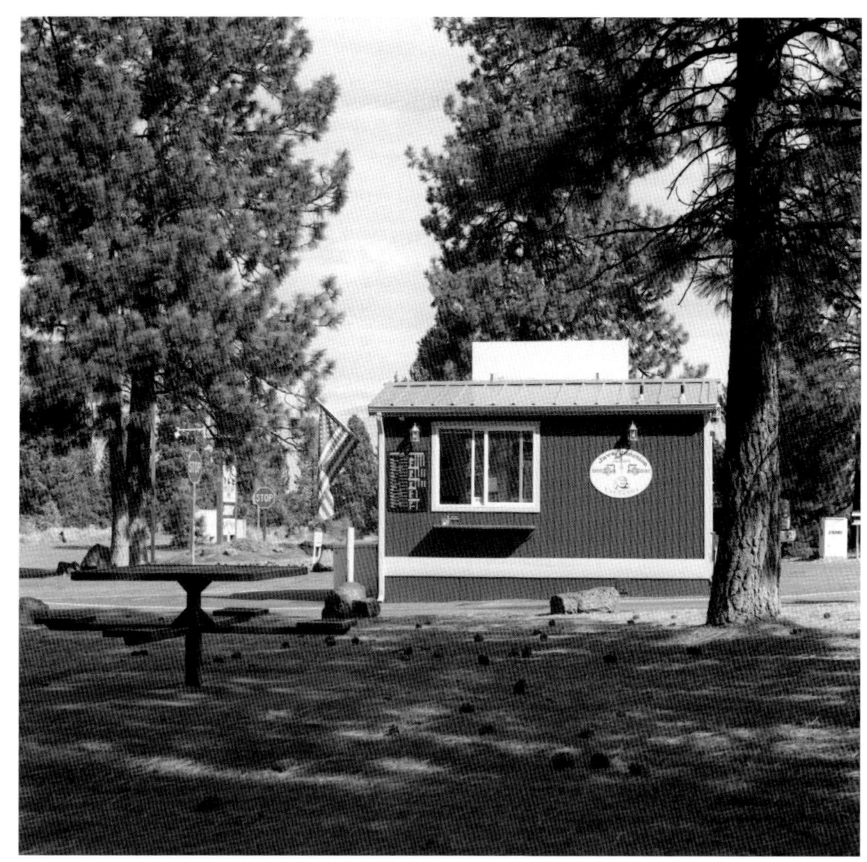

▲ *Java Junction, Bend, Oregon*

◂ *Outlaw Coffee, Prineville, Oregon*

portant event in the history of coffee. In 1600, Catholic priests wanted to ban coffee, proclaiming it "the devil's drink." This was more than a little related to the fact that coffee was introduced to eastern Europe by Muslim Arabs. Pope Clement VIII tried it, liked it, and said it was "so delicious that it would be a pity to let the infidels have exclusive use of it. We shall cheat Satan by baptizing it."

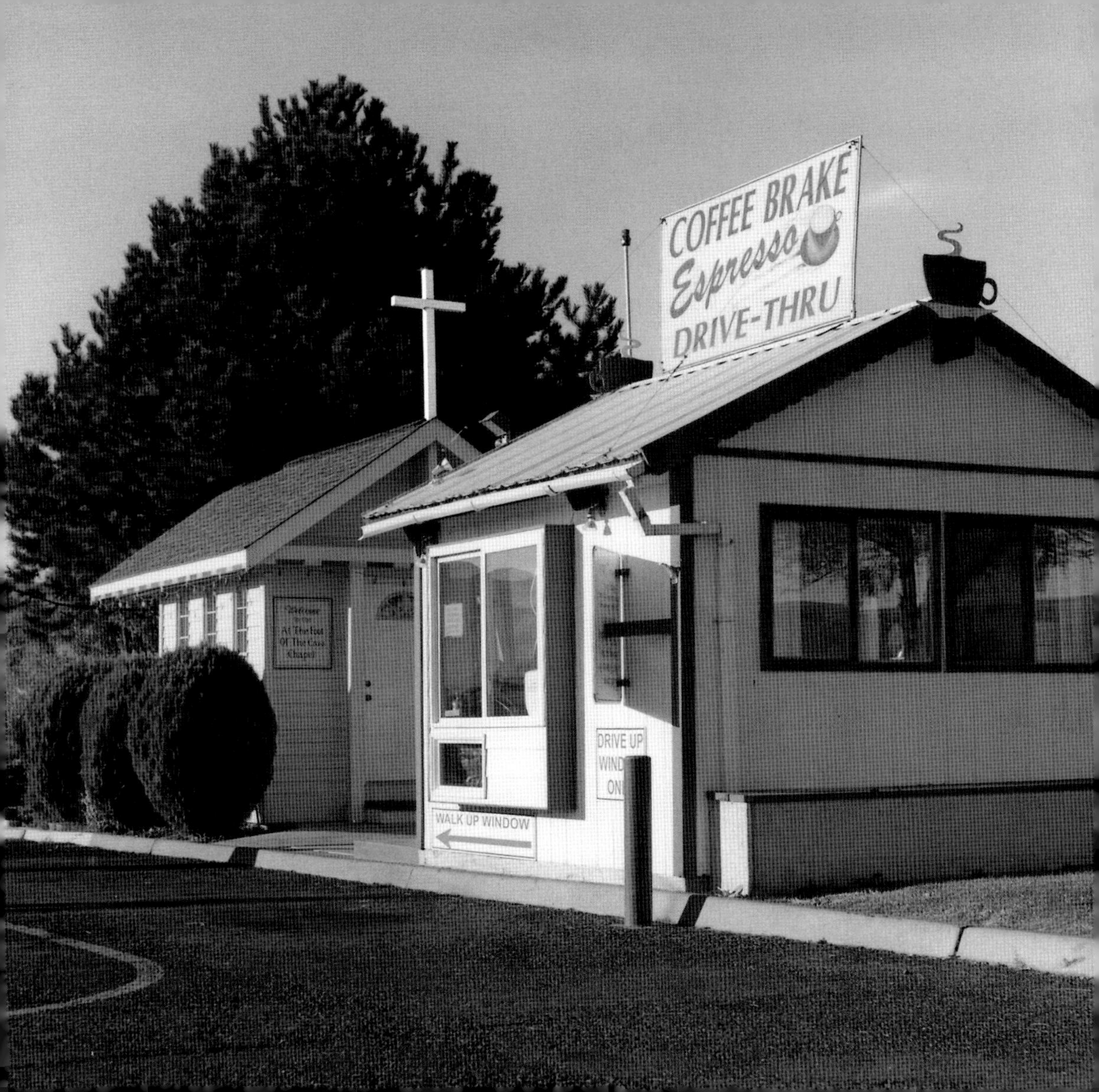
COFFEE BRAKE
Espresso
DRIVE-THRU
DRIVE UP
WALK UP WINDOW

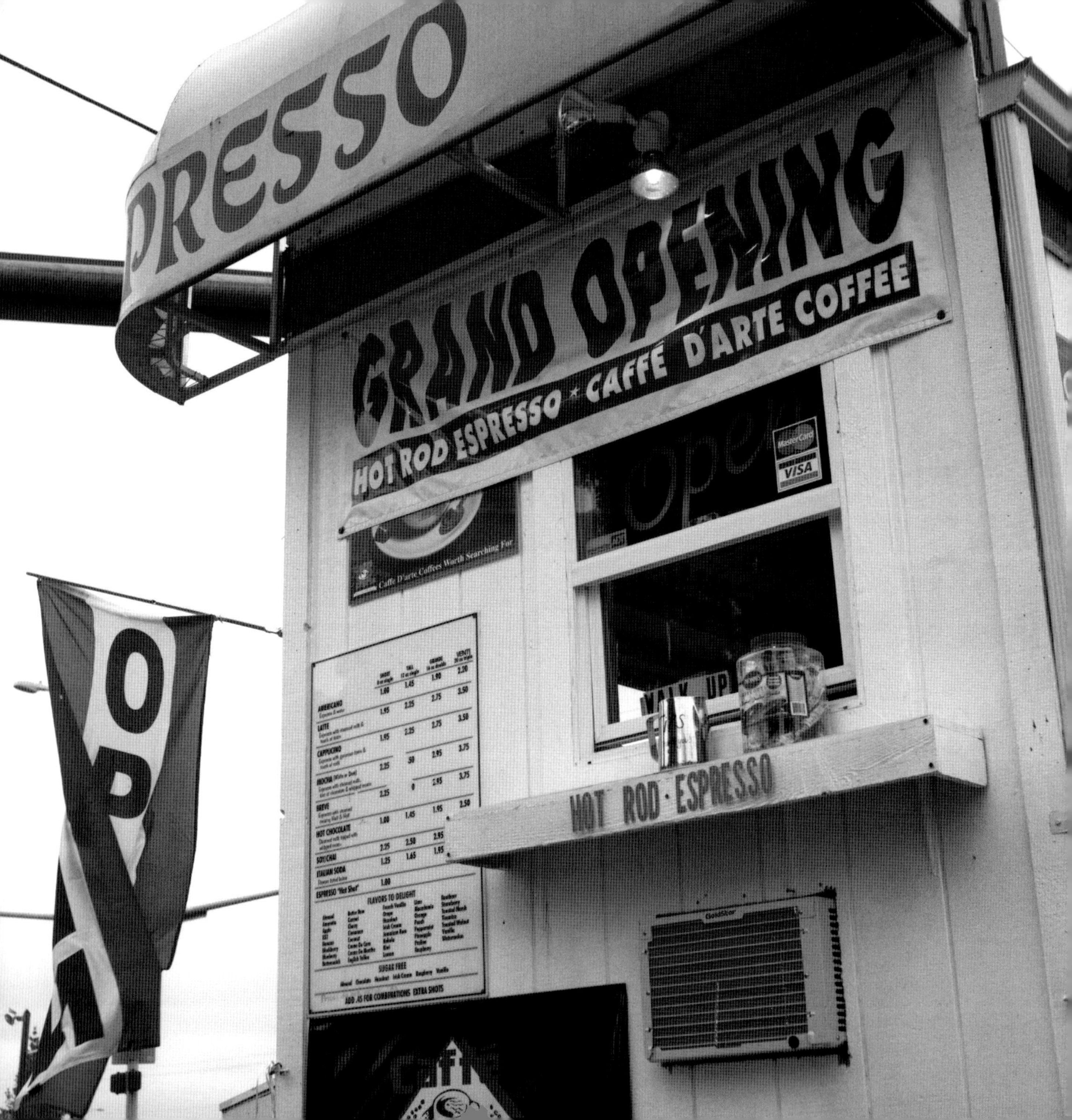
PRESSO
GRAND OPENING
HOT ROD ESPRESSO ★ CAFFÉ D'ARTE COFFEE
Open
MasterCard
VISA
Caffè D'Arte Coffees Worth Searching For
AMERICANO
LATTE
CAPPUCINO
MOCHA
BREVE
HOT CHOCOLATE
SOY CHAI
ITALIAN SODA
FLAVORS TO DELIGHT
SUGAR FREE
ADD .45 FOR COMBINATIONS EXTRA SHOTS
HOT ROD ESPRESSO
O
P

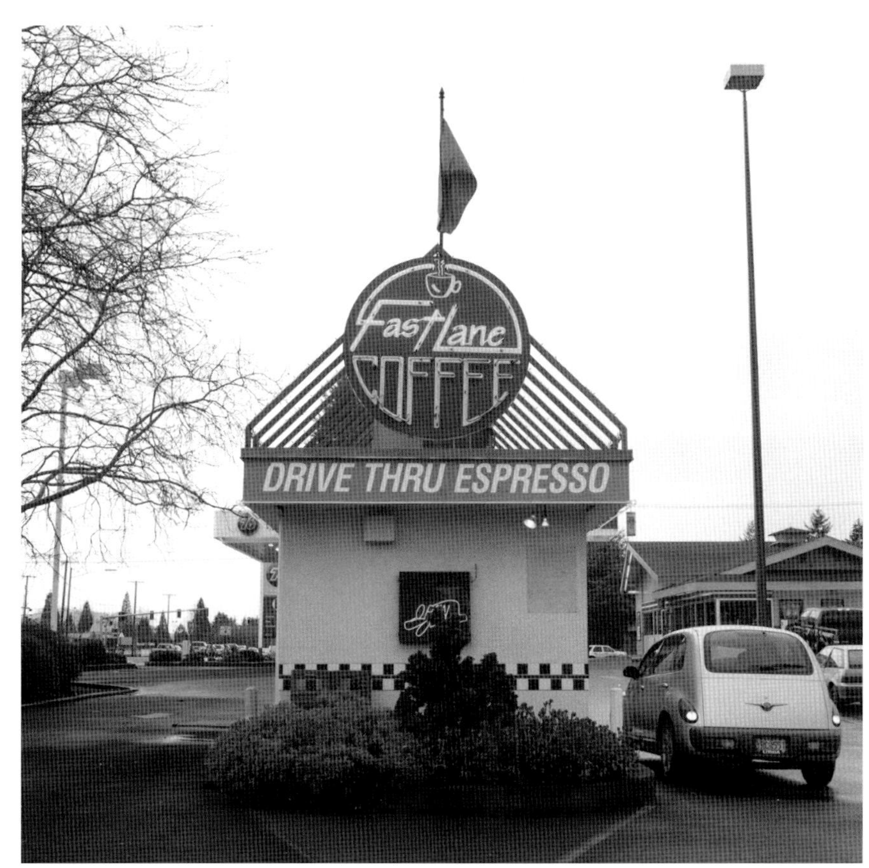

▲ *Fast Lane Coffee, Springfield, Oregon*

◂ *Hot Rod Espresso, Seattle, Washington*

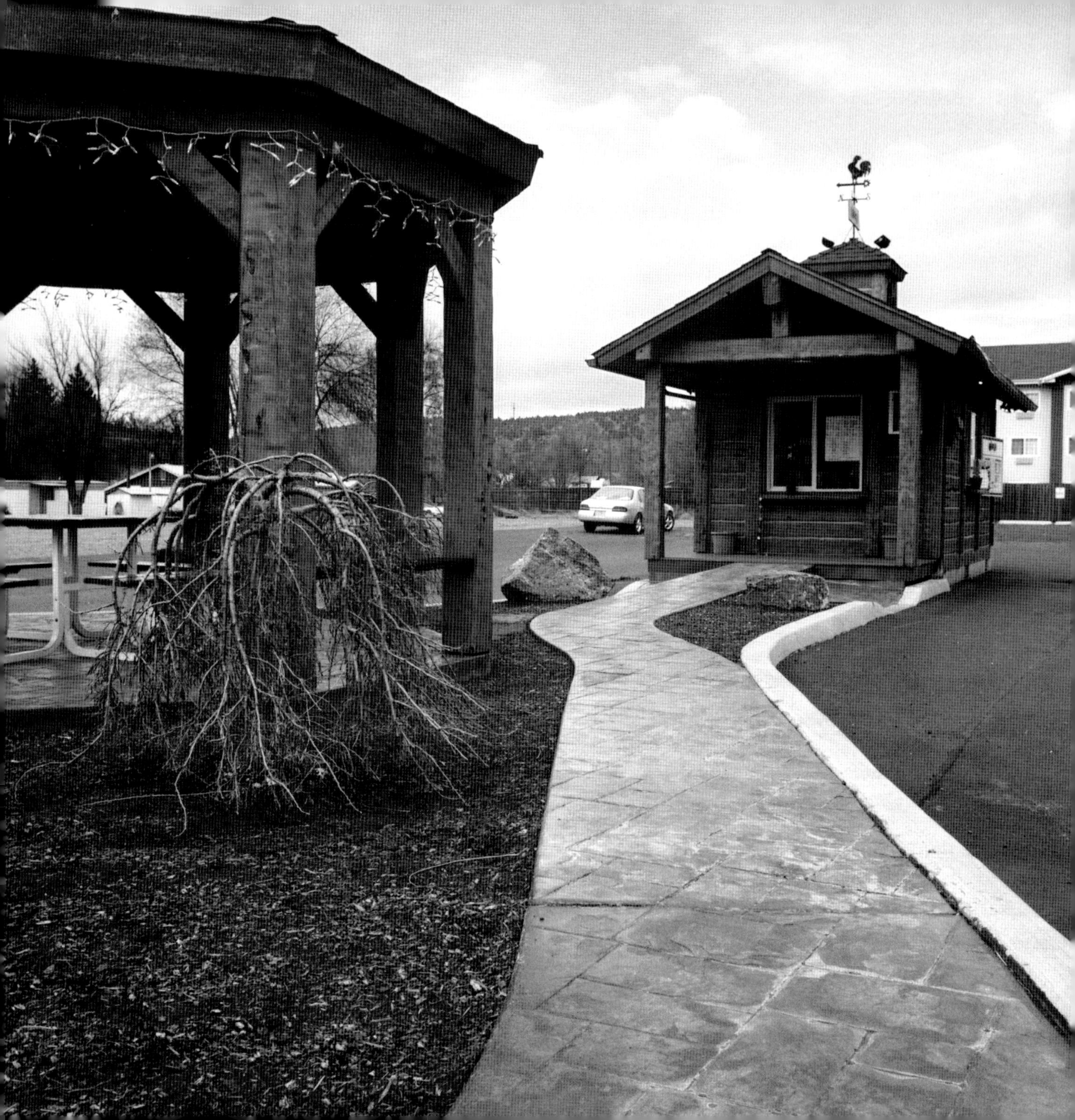

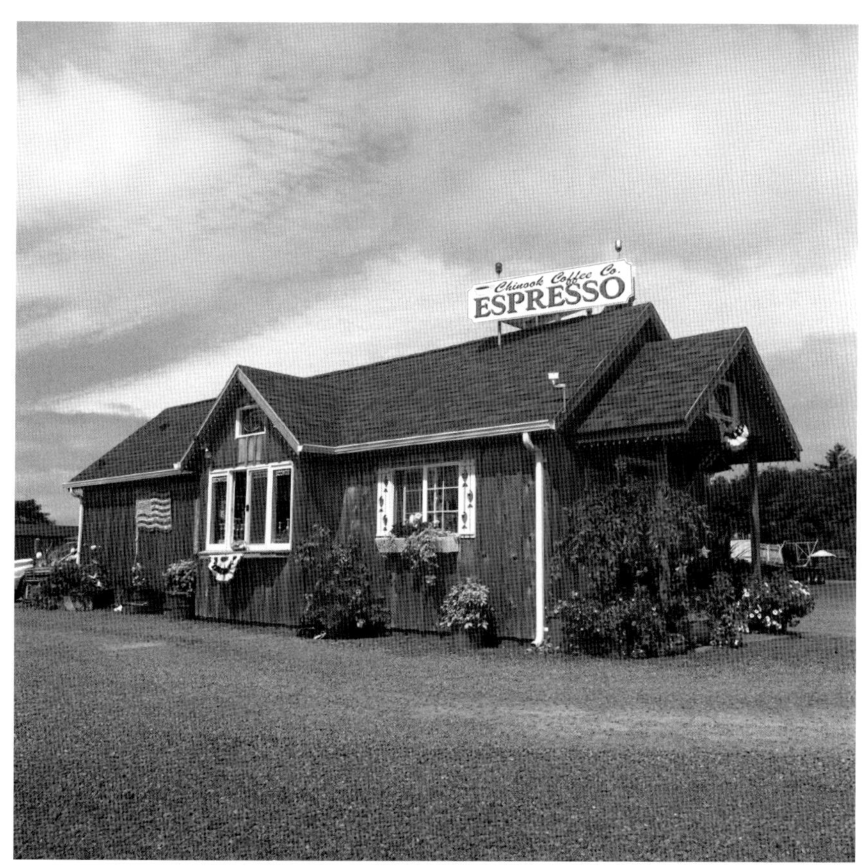

▲ *Chinook Coffee Co., Chinook, Washington*

◀ *Chick's, Prineville, Oregon*

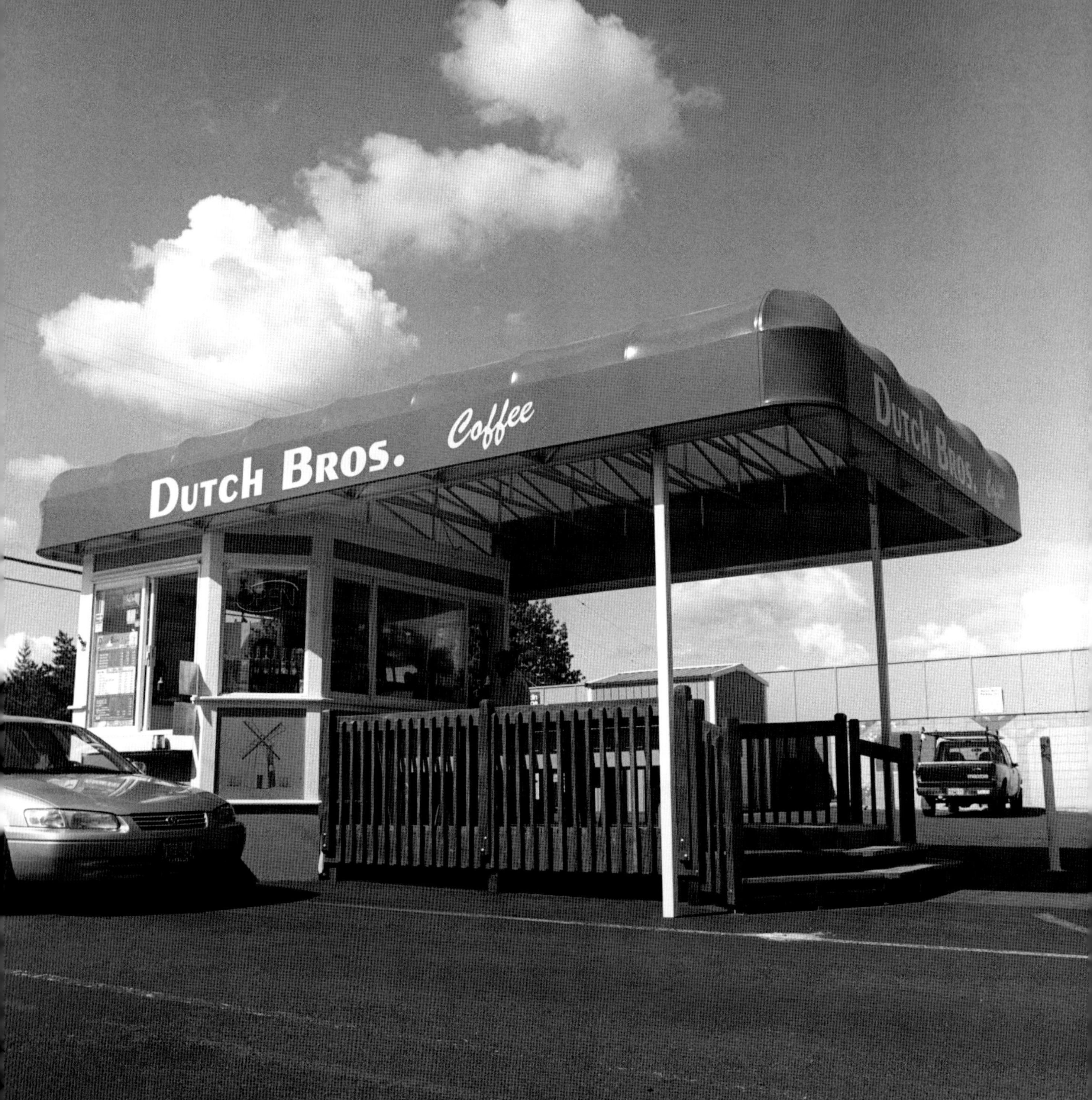
DUTCH BROS. Coffee
DUTCH BROS. Coffee

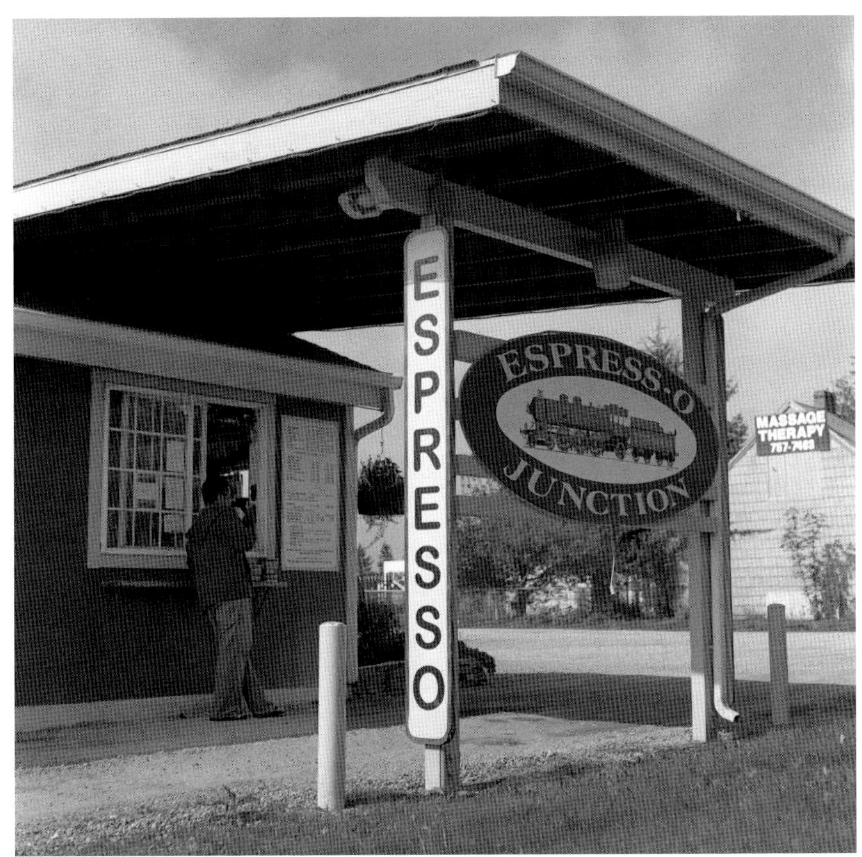

▲ *Espresso Junction, Burlington, Washington*

◂ *Dutch Bros. Coffee, Eugene, Oregon*

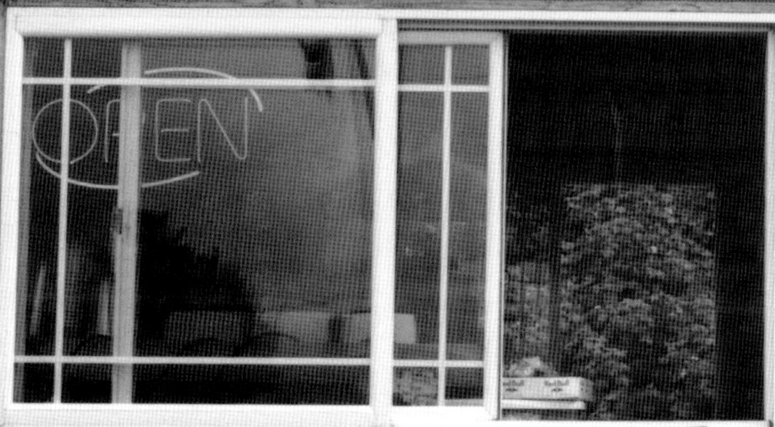
OPEN

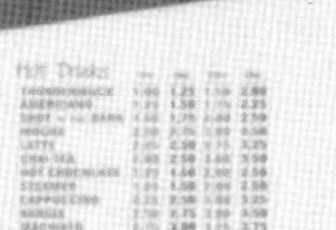
Daily Special

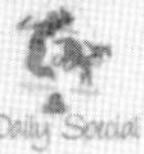

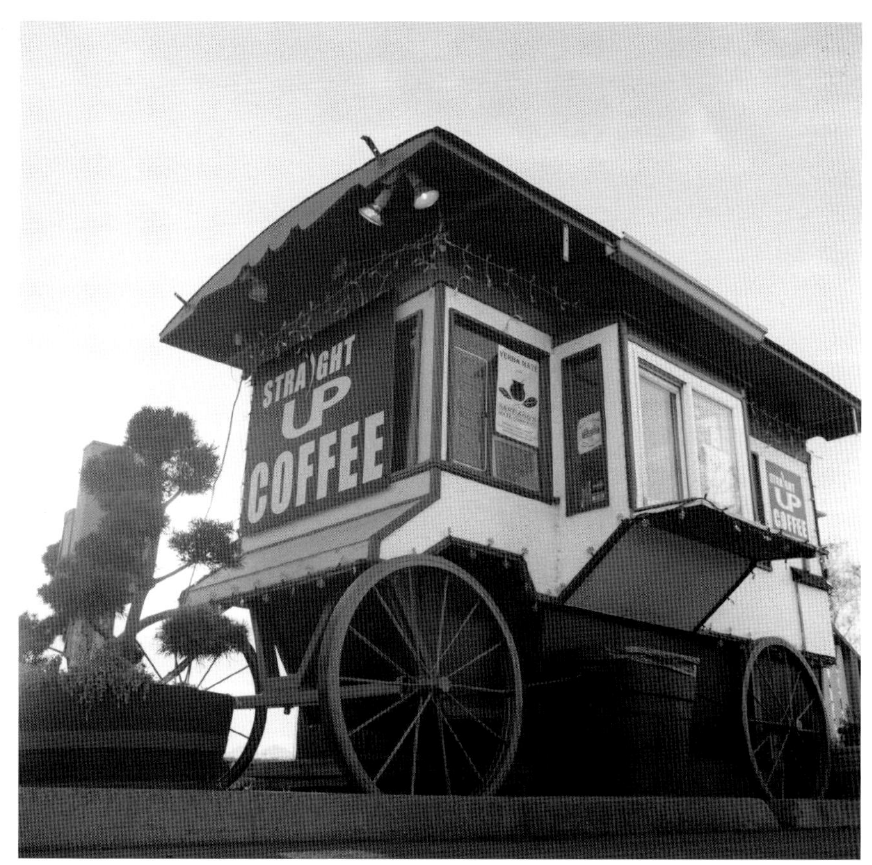

▲ Straight Up Coffee, *Redmond, Oregon*

◀ *Kick Ass Koffee, Astoria, Oregon*

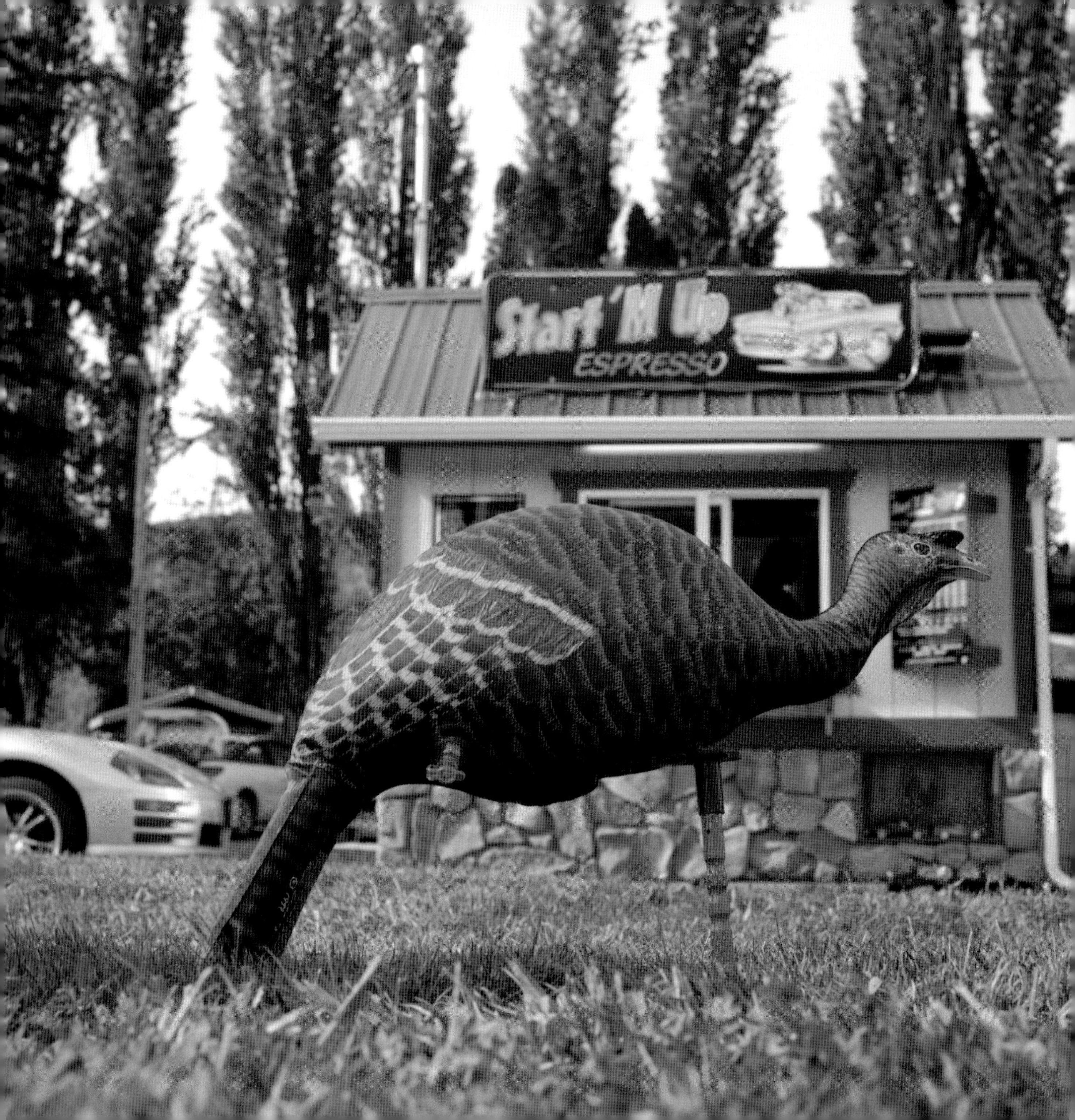
Start 'M Up
ESPRESSO

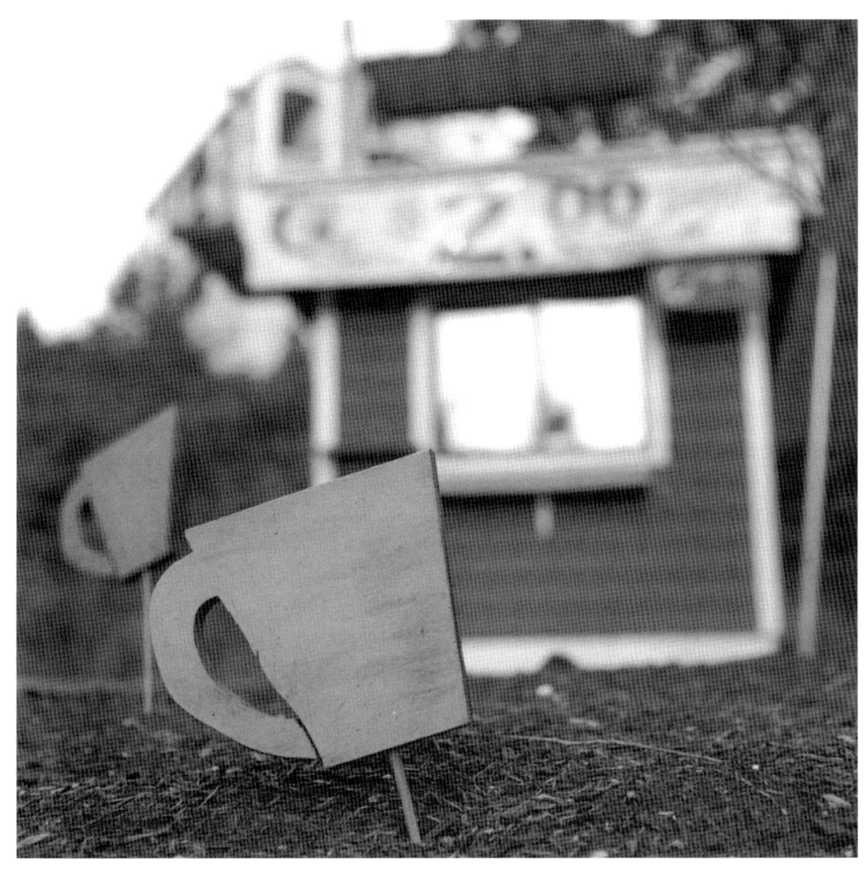

▲ *Oasis Coffee, Bothell, Washington*

◀ *Start 'M Up Espresso, Startup, Washington*

Red Cup Espresso, Maltby, Washington

Although it appears to be a soft-drink drive-through, this cup-shaped building actually serves espresso. Originally built by the owner of the Herfy's hamburger diner in Everett for $20,000, it was later moved to Maltby by Ron Nardone (who seemingly owns all of Maltby), and it now sits in front of the Maltby Cafe.

Constructed of wood and metal with a canvas roof, it has become a well-known landmark in southern Snohomish County.

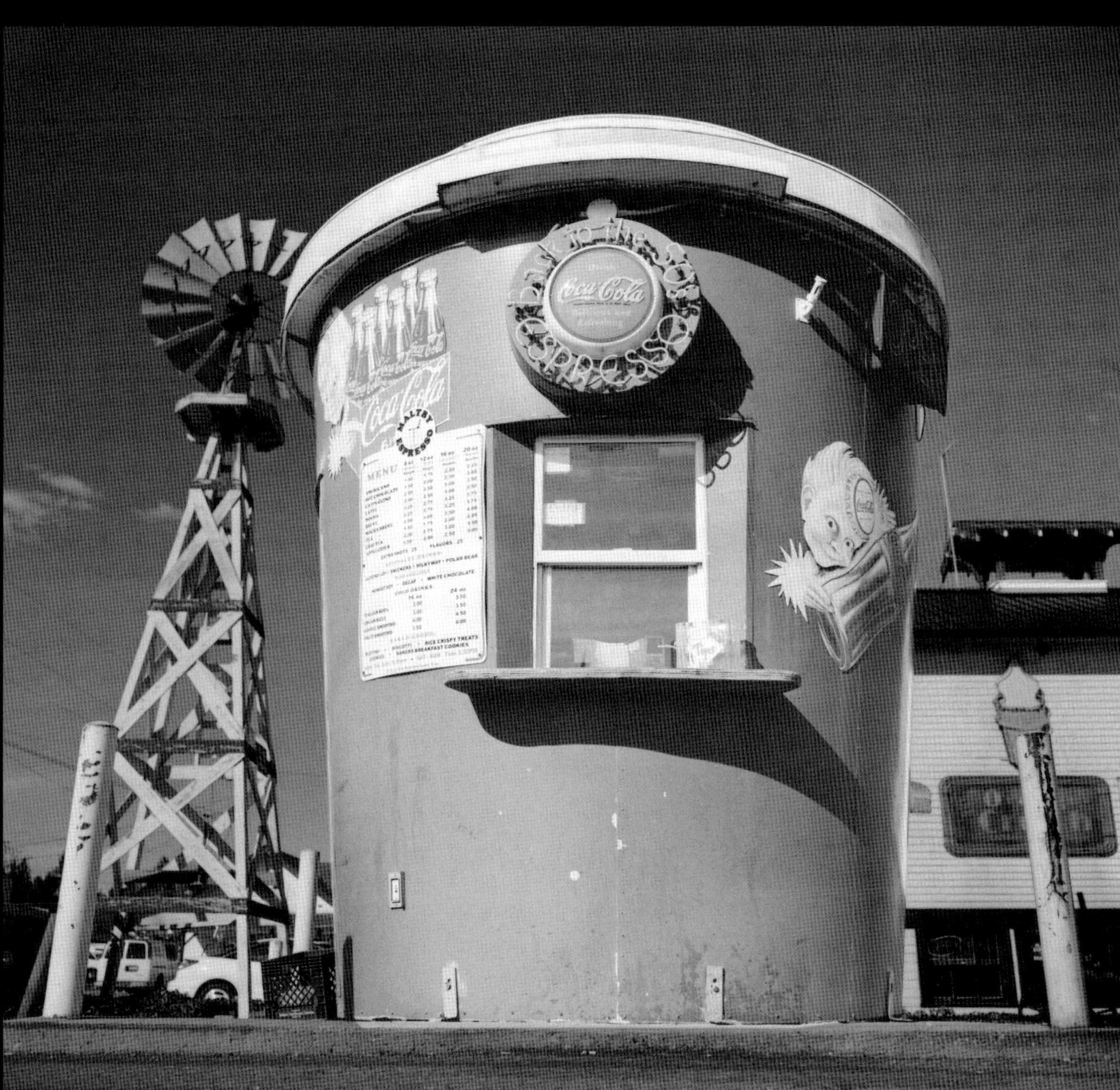
Coca-Cola
back to the
ESPRESSO
Coca-Cola
MALTSY ESPRESSO
MENU

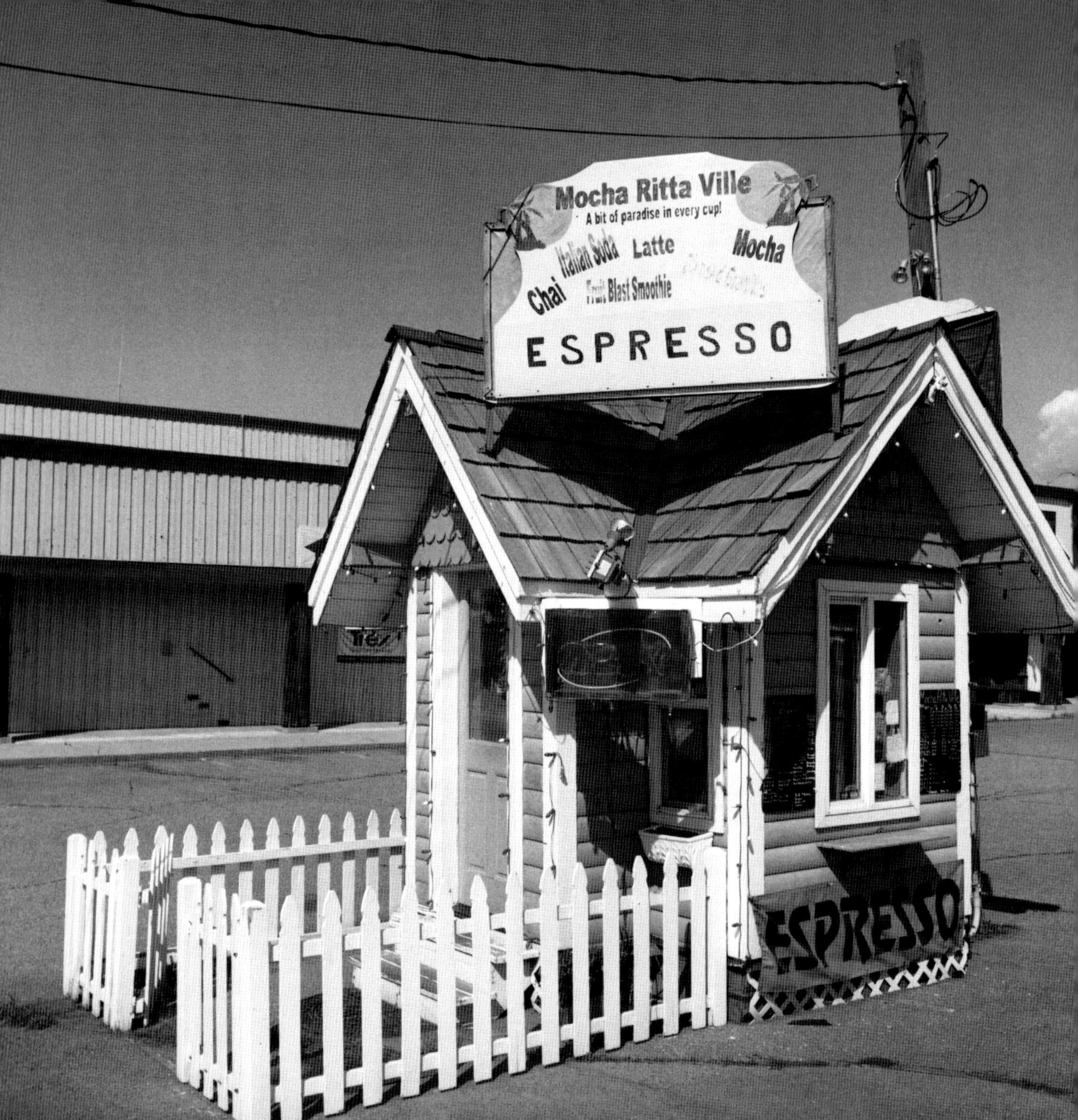
Mocha Ritta Ville
A bit of paradise in every cup!
Italian Soda
Latte
Mocha
Chai
Fruit Blast Smoothie
ESPRESSO
ESPRESSO

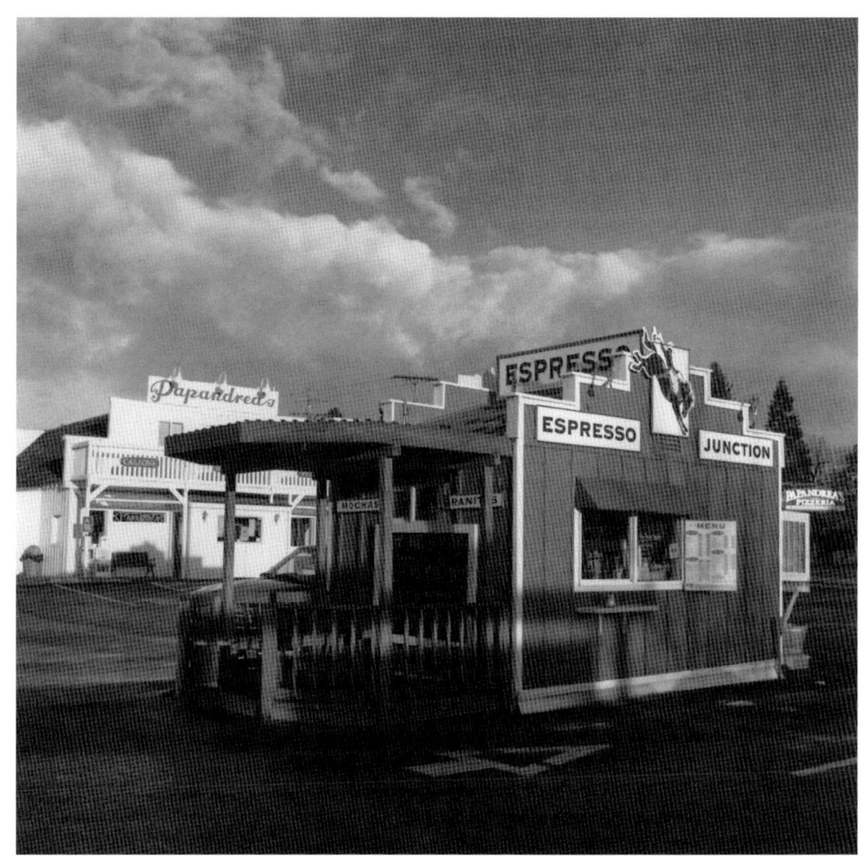

▲ *Espresso Junction, Sisters, Oregon*

◀ *Mocha Ritta Ville, Coeur d'Alene, Idaho*

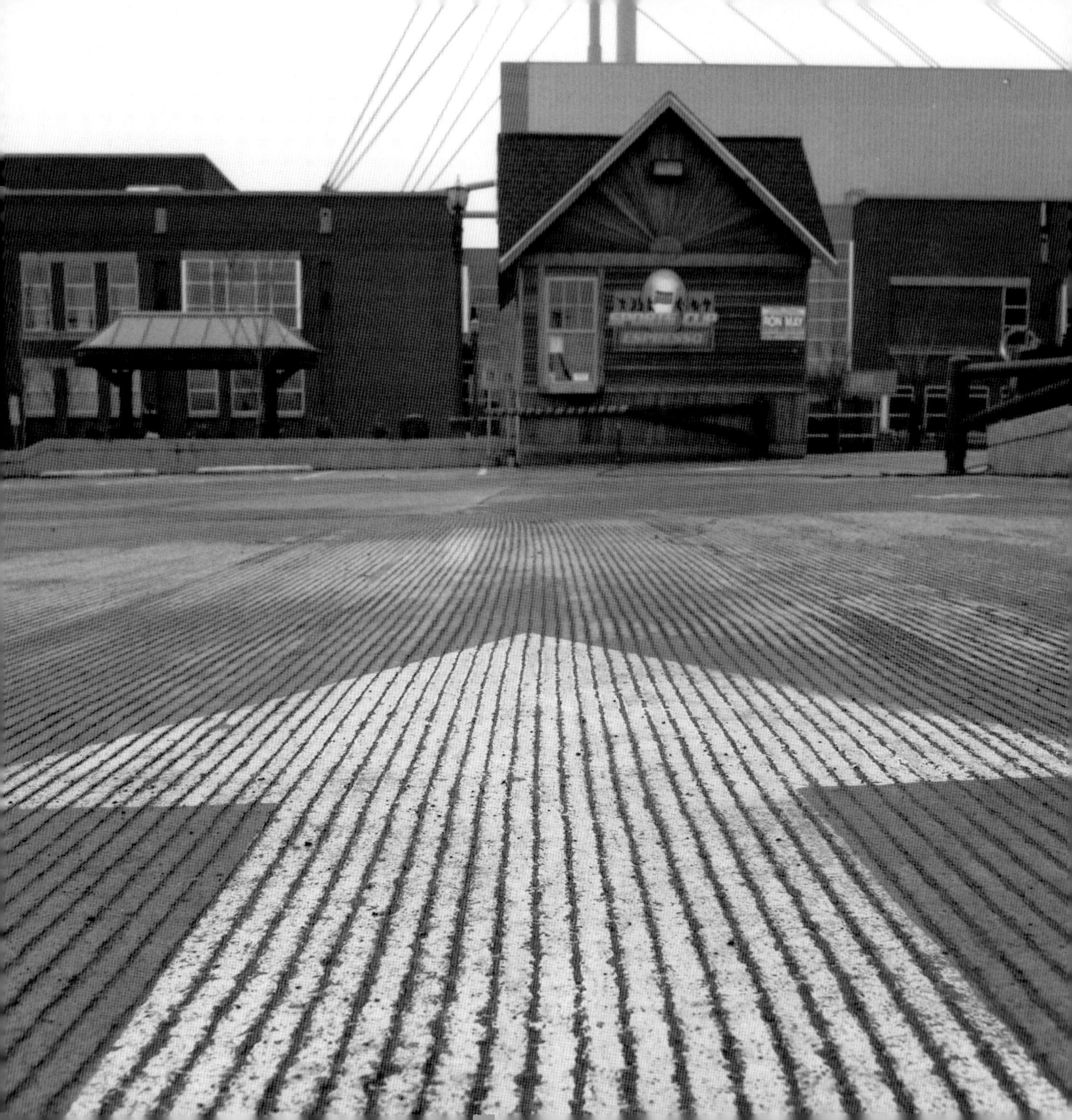

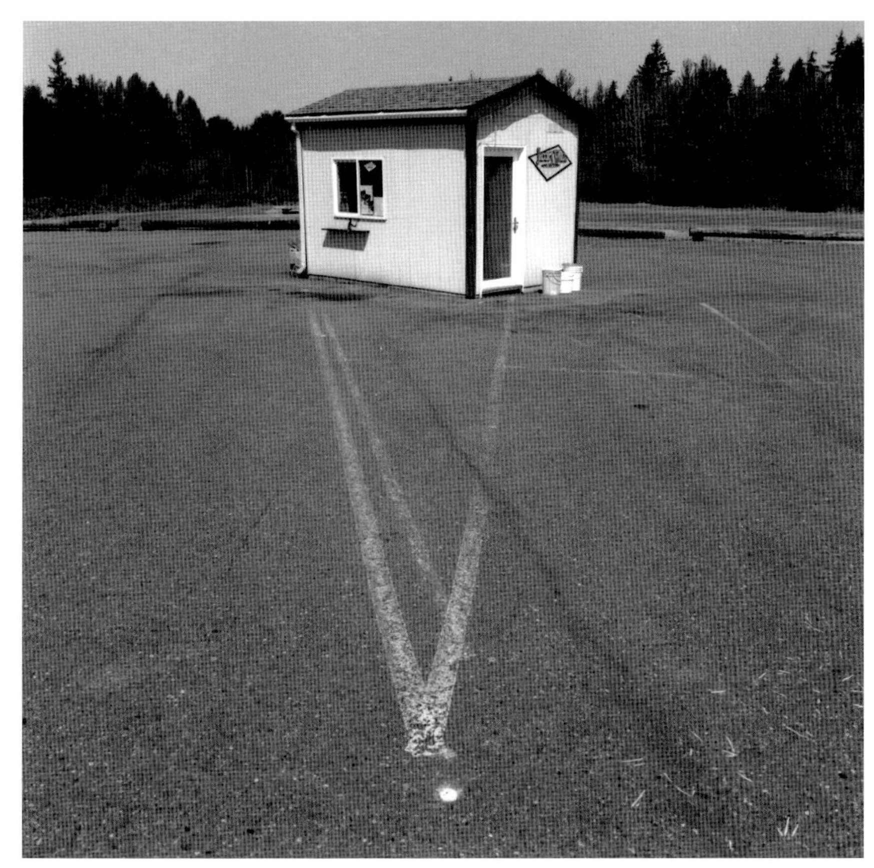

▲ *Jacob's Well and outreach ministry of Park Ridge Community Church, Bothell, Washington*

◄ *Sports Cup Espresso, Everett, Washington*

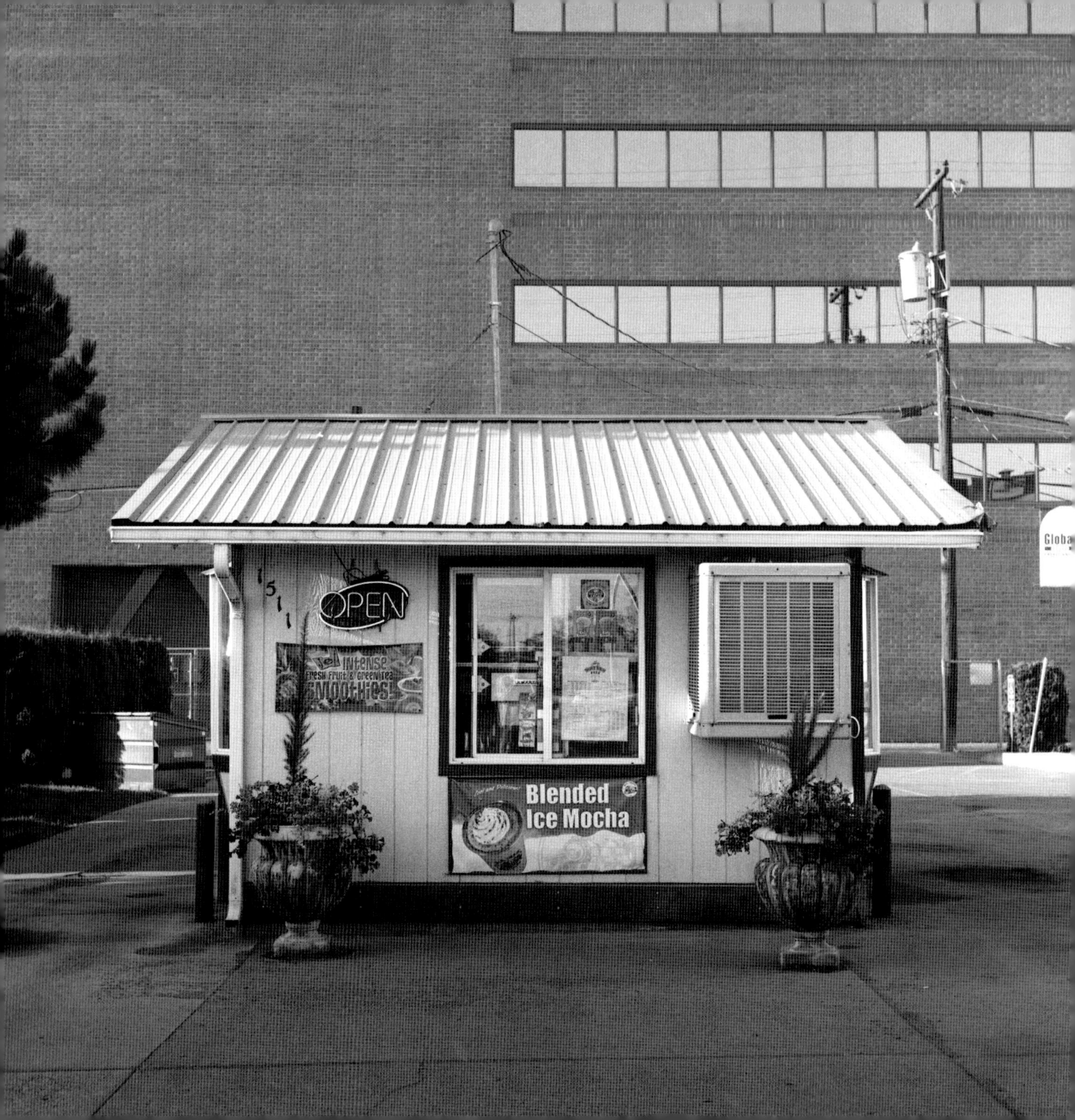
1511
OPEN
Intense
Fresh Fruit & Green Tea
Smoothies!
Blended
Ice Mocha

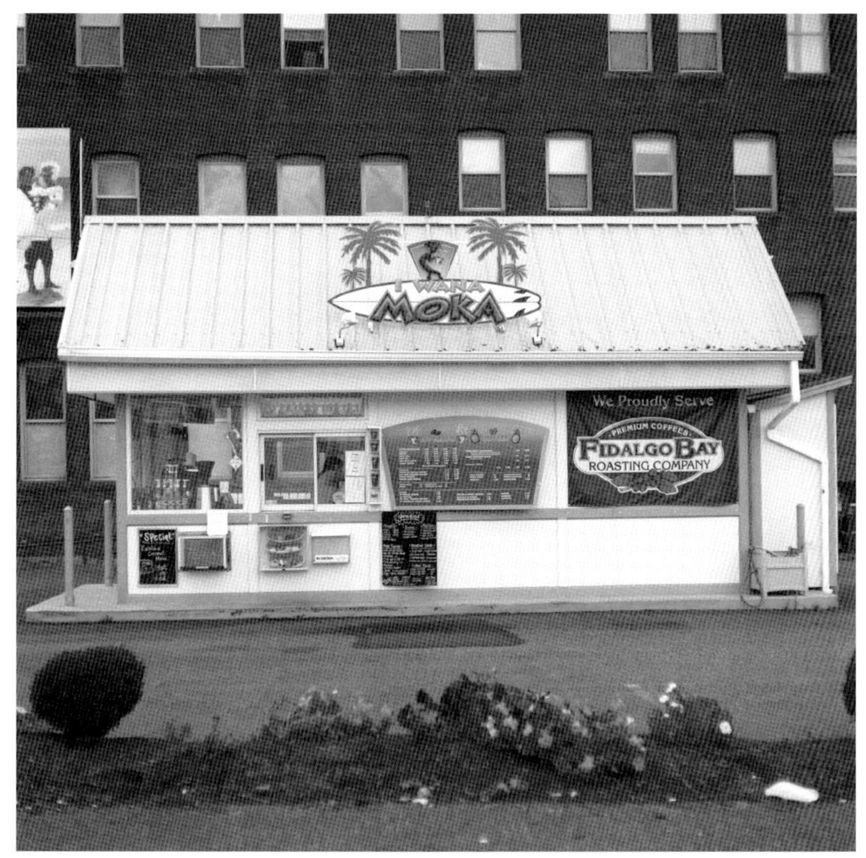

▲ *I Wana Moka, Bellingham, Washington*

◂ *Walnut Street Espresso, Spokane, Washington*

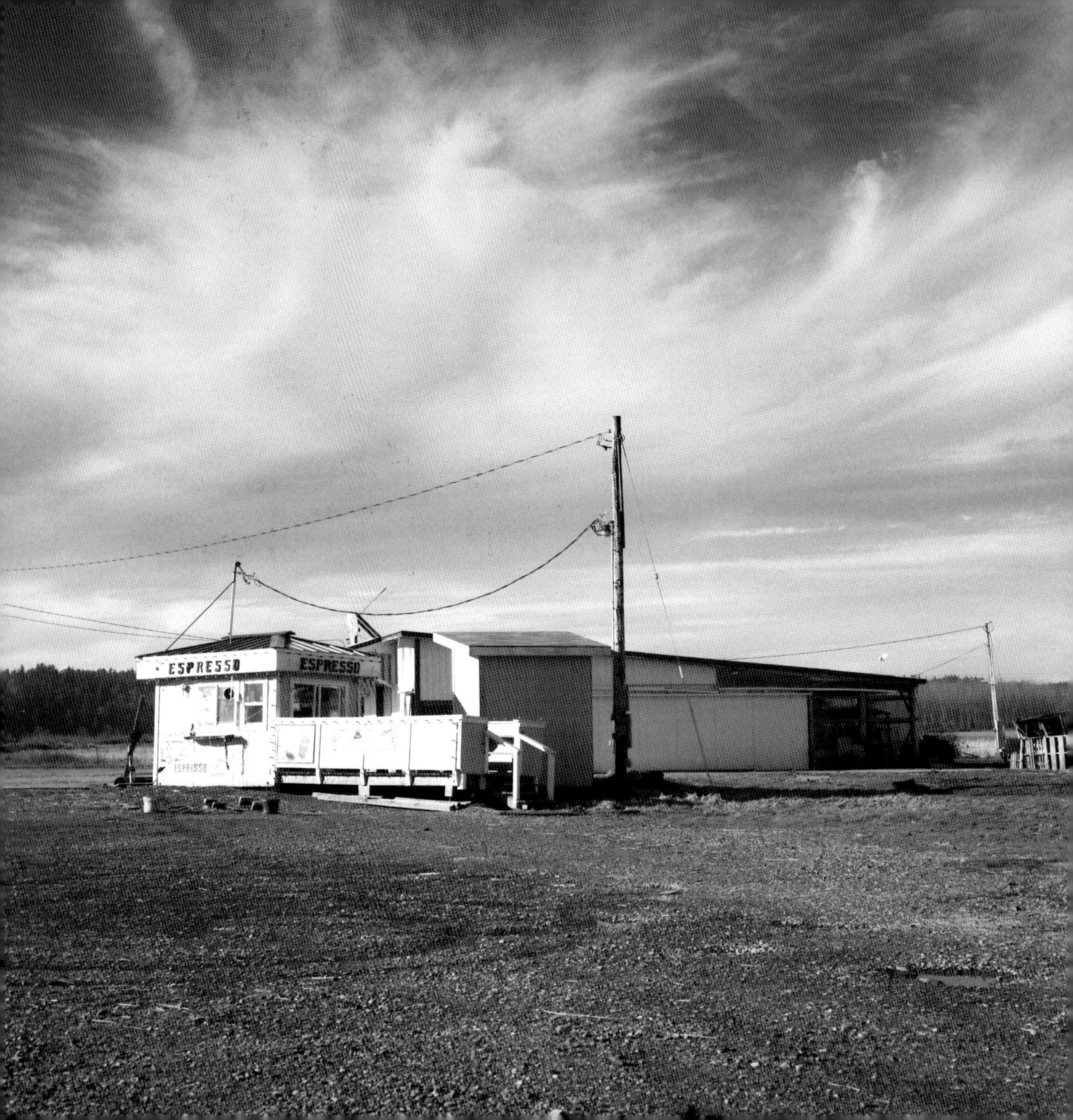
ESPRESSO
ESPRESSO
ESPRESSO

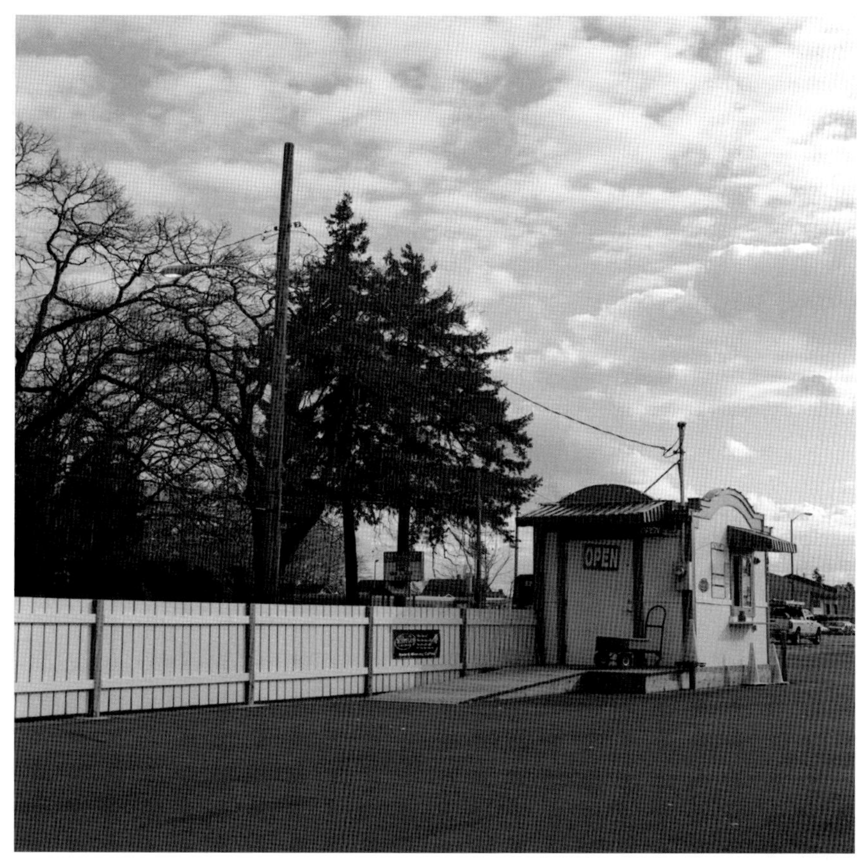

▲ *Emerald Bay Espresso, Tacoma, Washington*

◄ *Unoccupied, Ebey Island, near Everett, Washington*

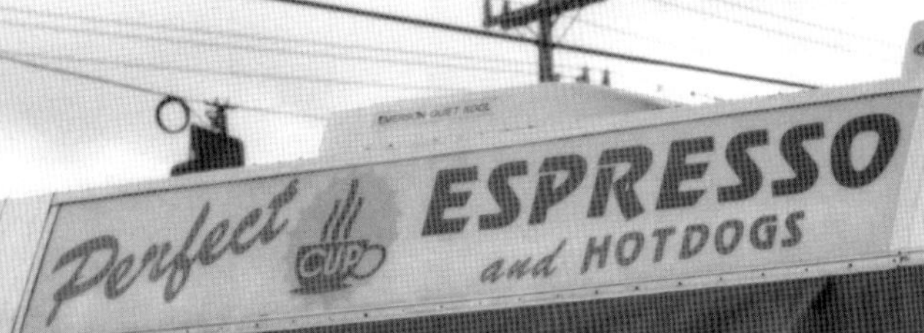
Perfect
CUP
ESPRESSO
and HOTDOGS

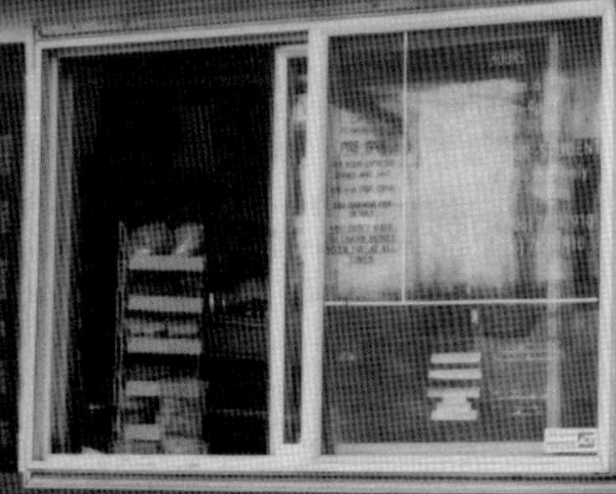
Drink Prices
Blended Drinks
SMOOTHIES
BIG TRAIN MOCHA
BIG TRAIN VANILLA LATTE
MOCHA SHAKES
FLAVORED MILK SHAKES
BLENDED CHAI TEA & MORE
Healthy Choices
GREEN TEA SMOOTHIE
LOW CARB DRINKS
LOW CARB PASTRY
PROTEIN SHAKE
House Favorite/Granita
ESPRESSO LATTE SLUSH
ESPRESSO MOCHA SLUSH
ESPRESSO FLAVORED
16 oz $4.00
20 oz $4.50
24 oz $5.00
32 oz $7.00
JUICE. TEA. ENERGY.

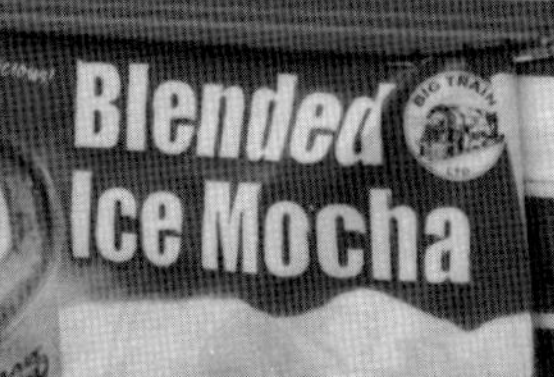
Blended
Ice Mocha

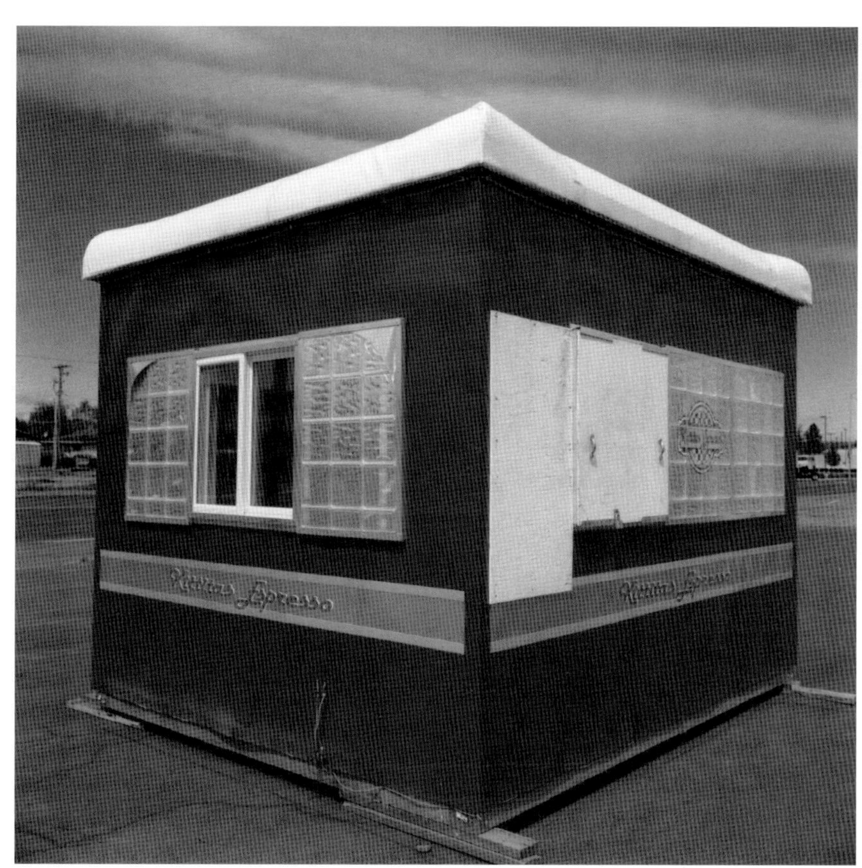

▲ *Kittitas Espresso, Quincy, Washington*

◂ *Perfect Espresso, Seattle, Washington*

Filling Station Espresso, Olympia, Washington

This building at Plum Street and Fourth Avenue in Olympia housed a filling station until the early 1980s. After a decade of vacancy, it was converted to a drive-through espresso stand in 1994. Although much smaller than other conversions of this type, it features glass windows on all four sides, allowing for a more natural and personal interaction between baristas and customers.

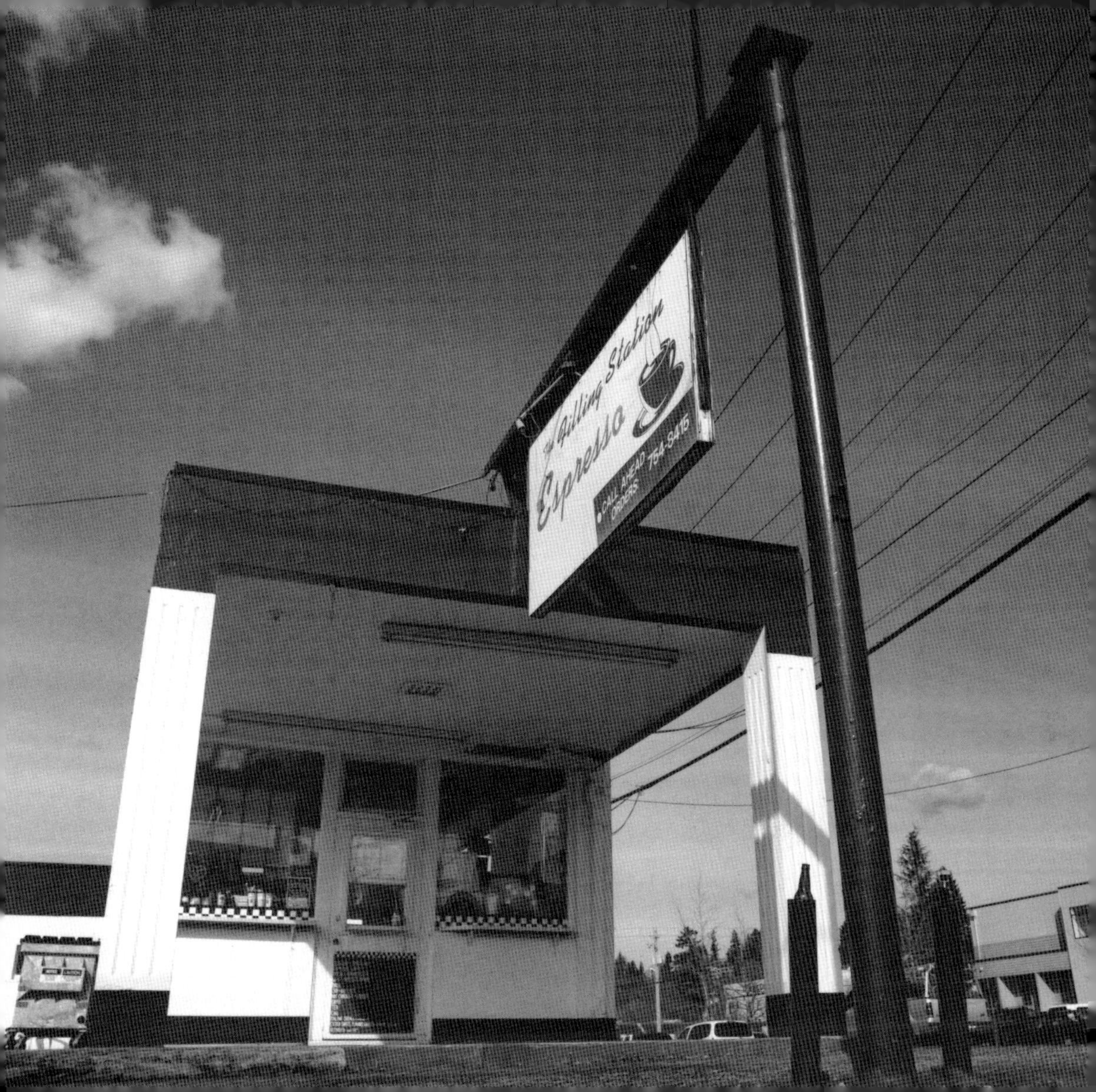
Filling Station
Espresso
CALL AHEAD ORDERS
754-8415

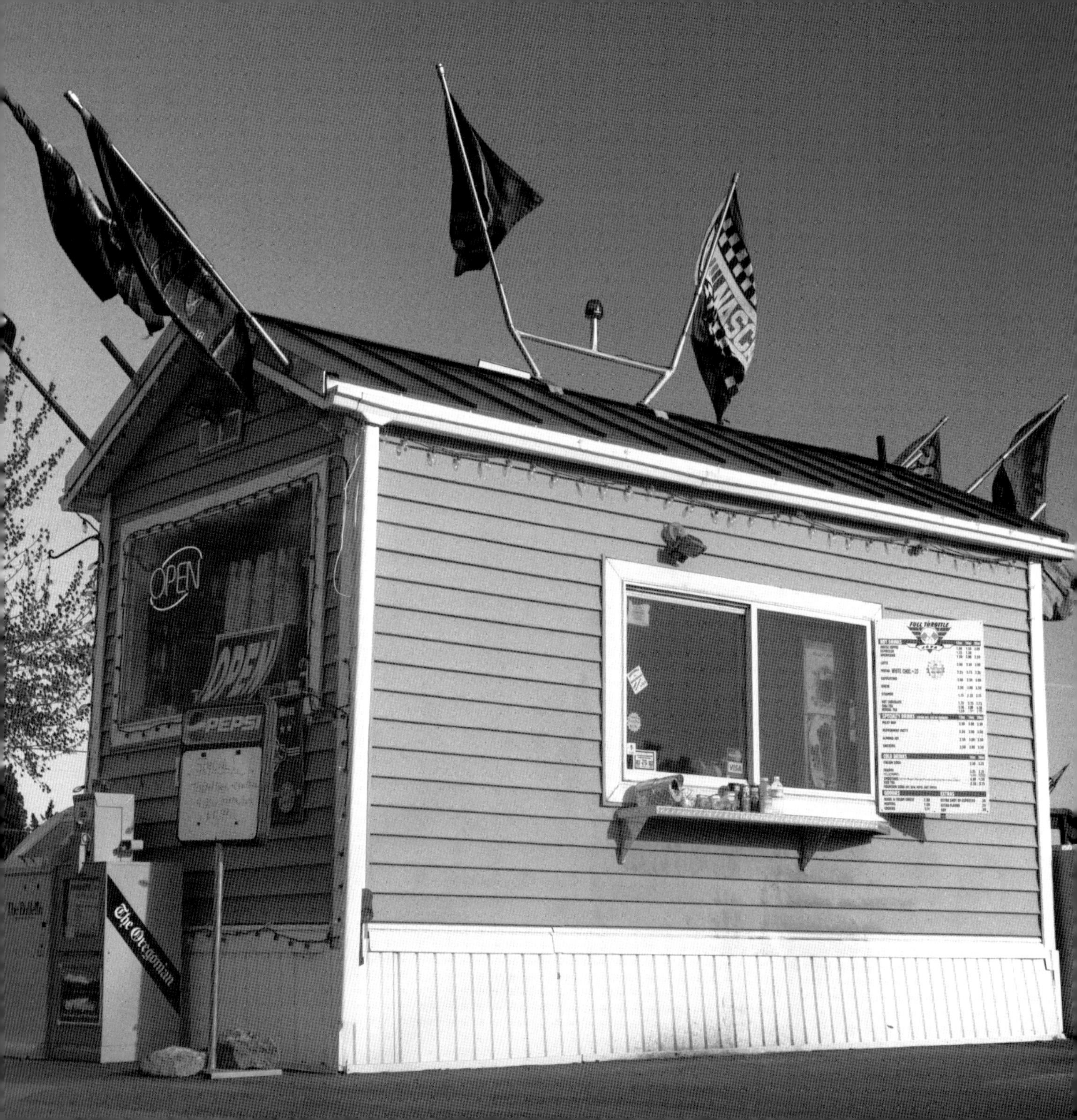
OPEN
OPEN
The Oregonian

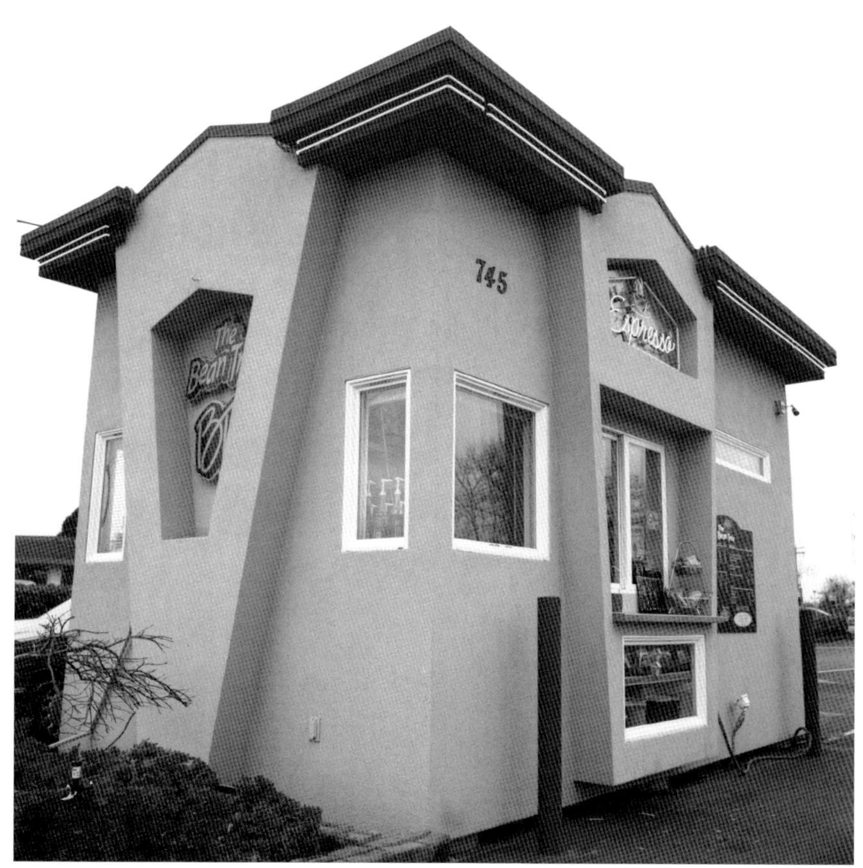

▲ *Bean Tree Espresso, Puyallup, Washington*

◂ *Full Throttle Java, Redmond, Oregon*

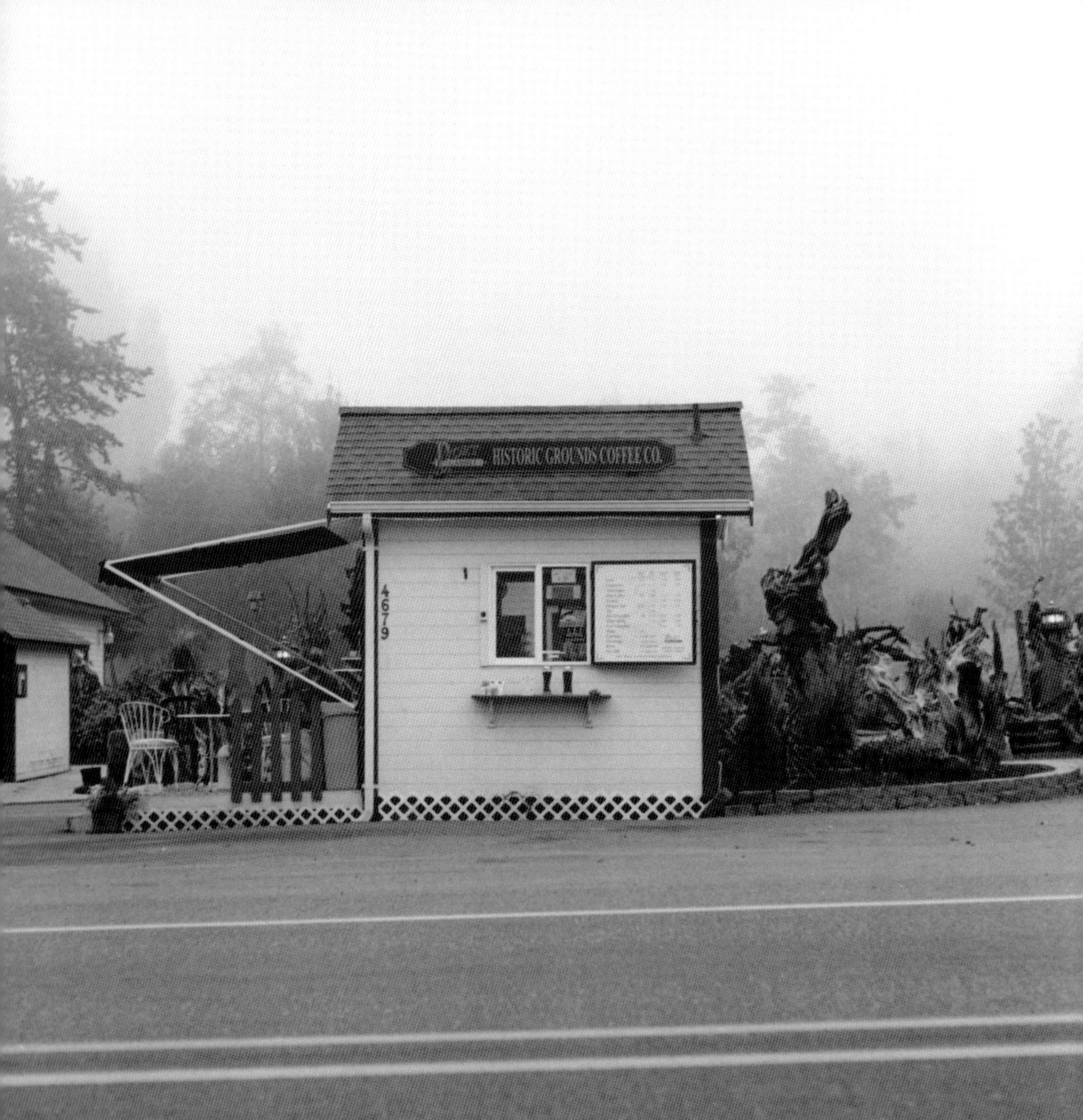
HISTORIC GROUNDS COFFEE CO.
4679

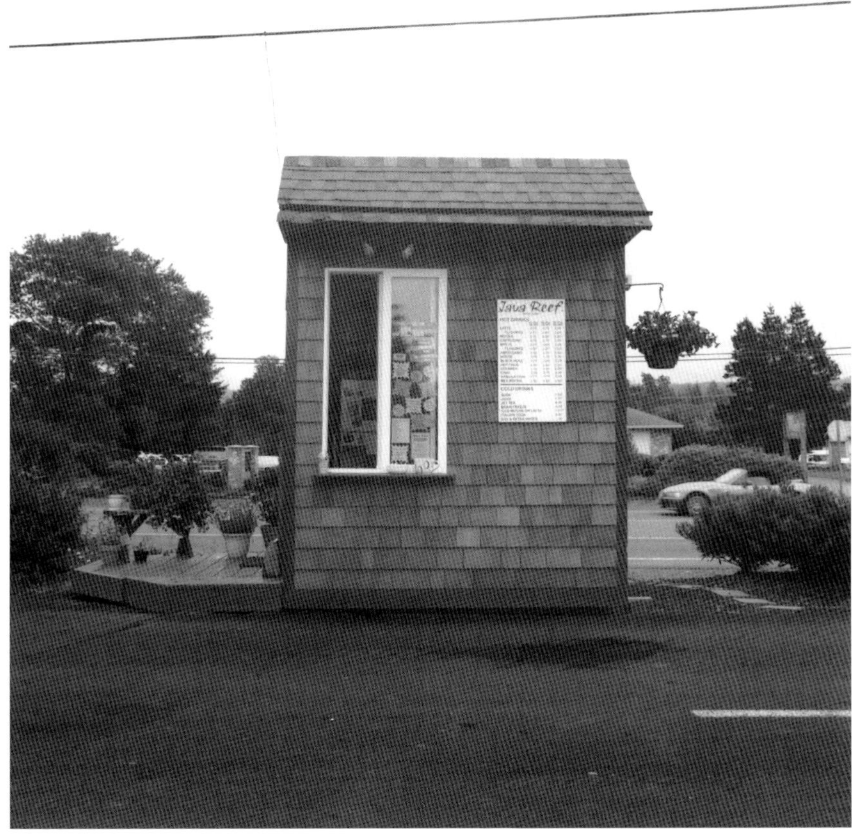

▲ *Java Reef, Seaside, Oregon*

◀ *Historic Grounds Coffee, Port Gamble, Washington*

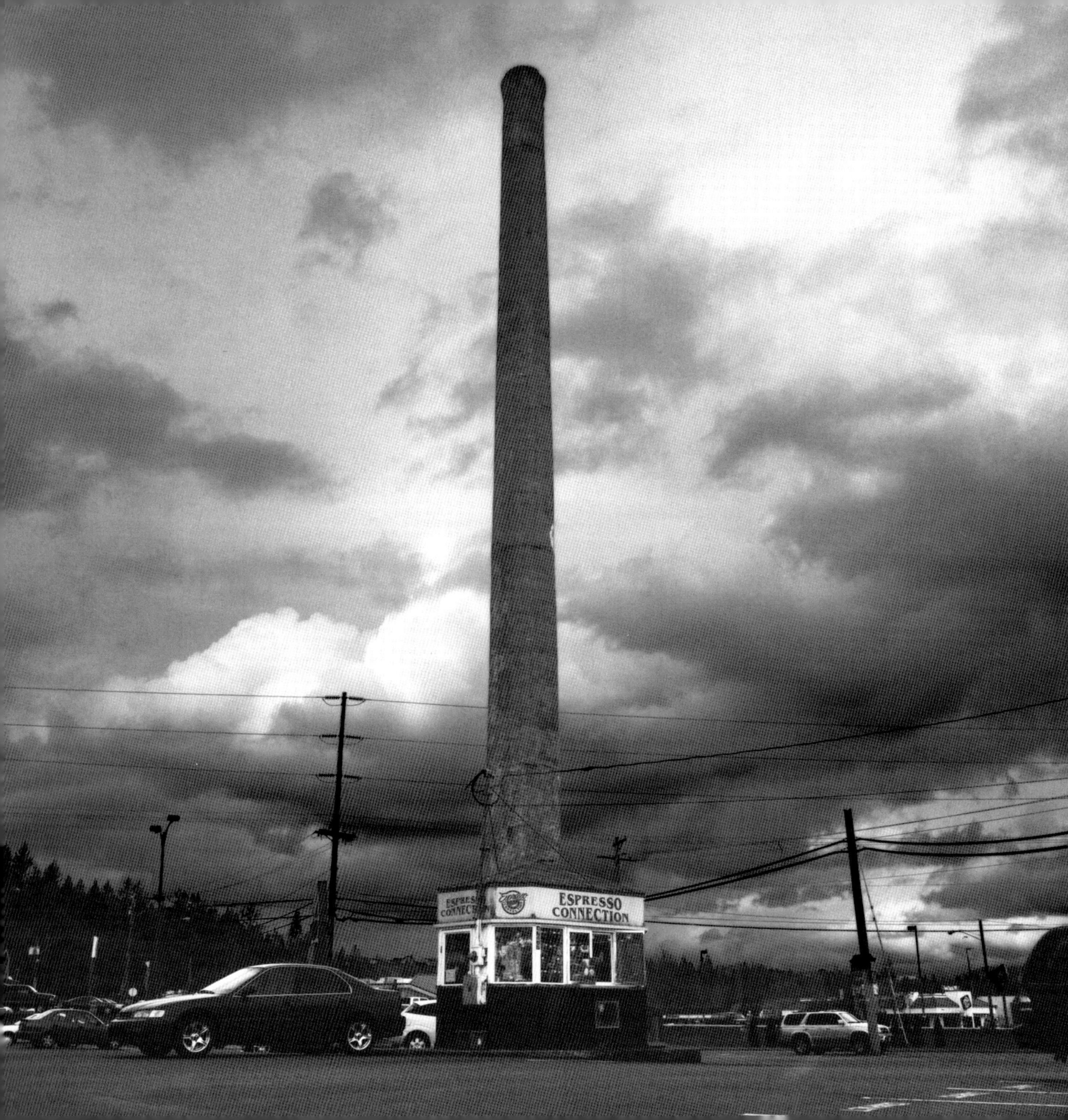
ESPRESSO
CONNECTION
ESPRESSO
CONNECTION

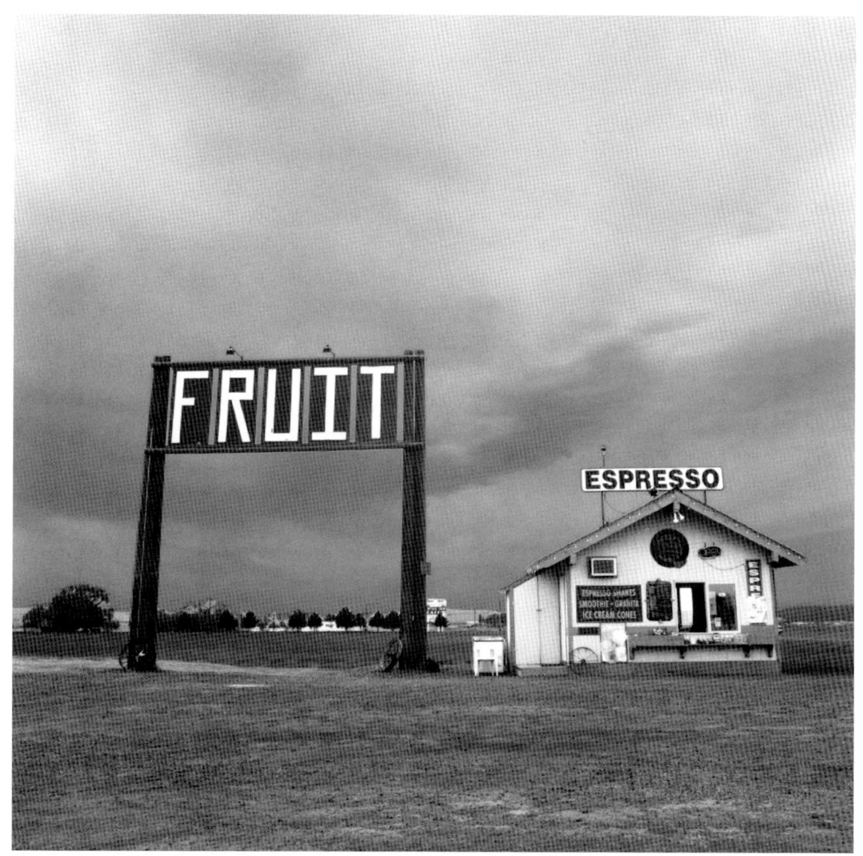

▲ *Elke's Espresso Etc., George, Washington*

◂ *Espresso Connection, Monroe, Washington*

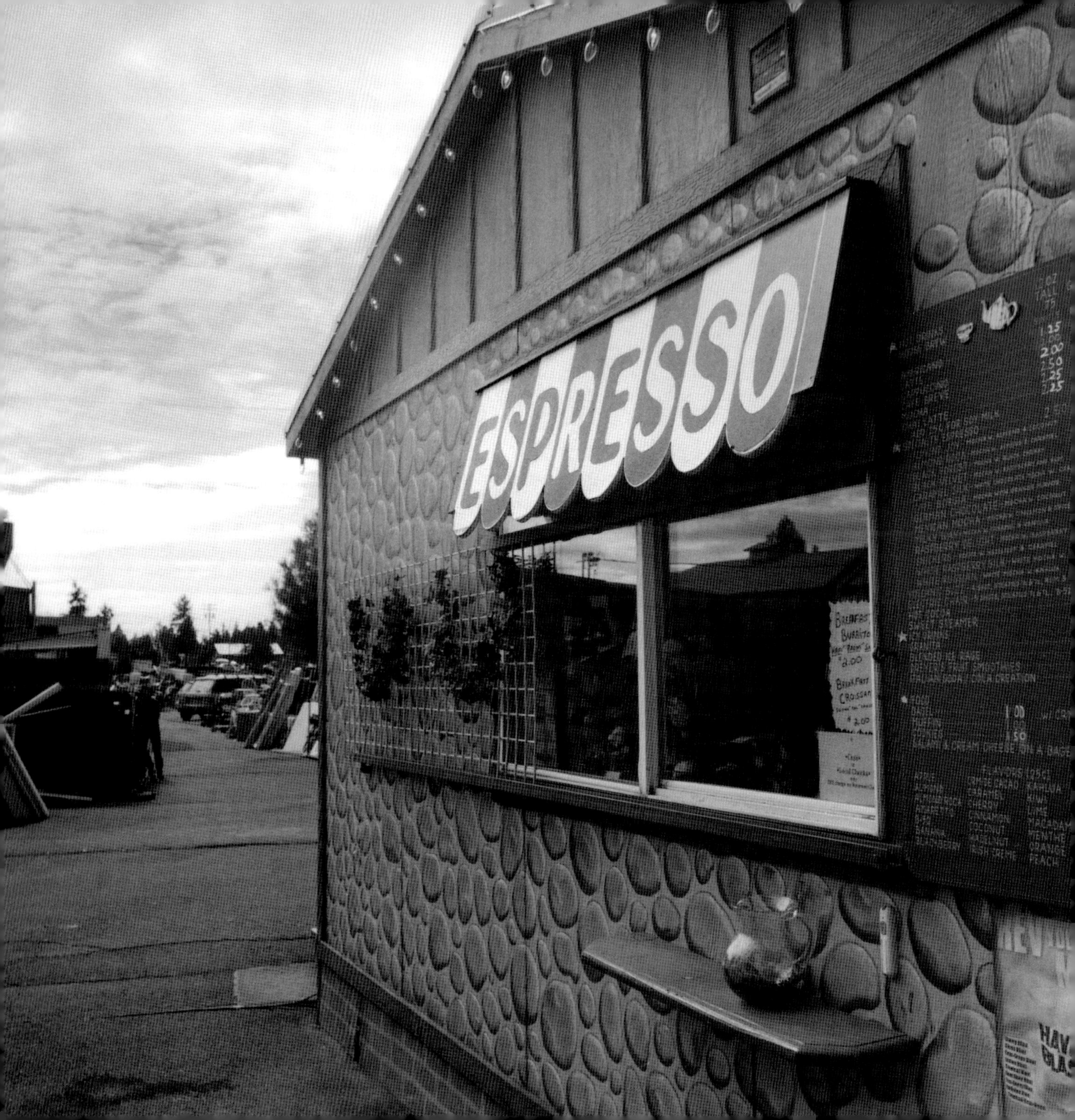
ESPRESSO

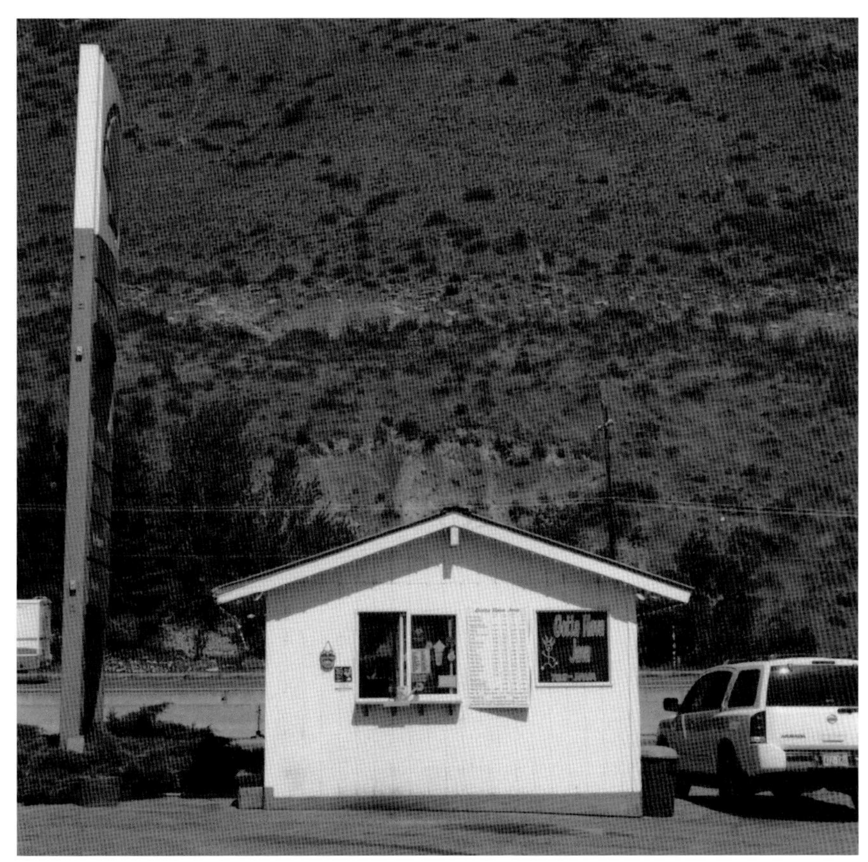

▲ *Gotta Hava Java, Cashmere, Washington*

◀ *Buz Stop, Bend, Oregon*

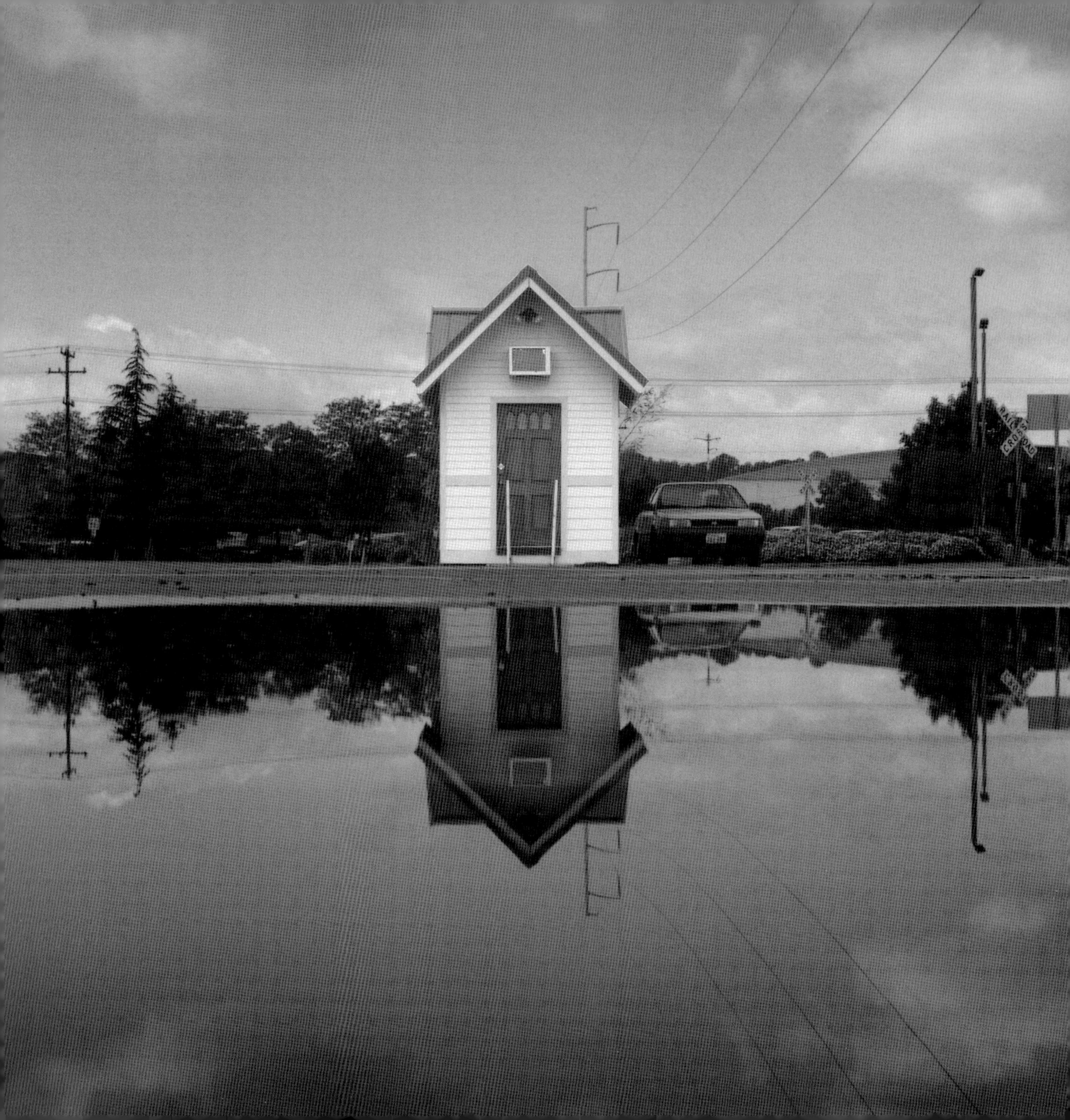

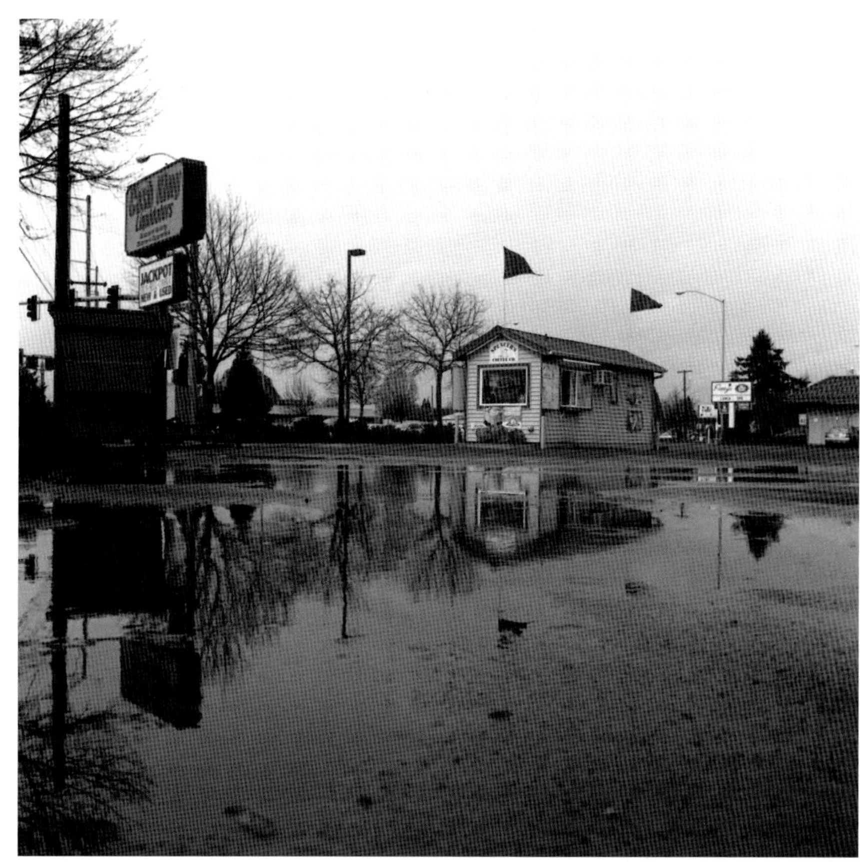

▲ *Spencer's Coffee Co., Eugene, Oregon*

◂ *Unoccupied, Seattle, Washington*

Gold Rush Coffee, *Eureka, California*

Joe and Karen Paff, owners of Gold Rush Coffee, use a solar electric system and a solar hot-water system at this drive-through, saving them approximately 25 percent on their electricity bills. Designed by Oakland architect, Joel Miroglio, it received a design award from *Metal Architecture Magazine* in 1999. The shiny metal building loosely resembles a giant tin can, although the surface is actually galvanized metal that has developed a beautiful patina over the past decade.

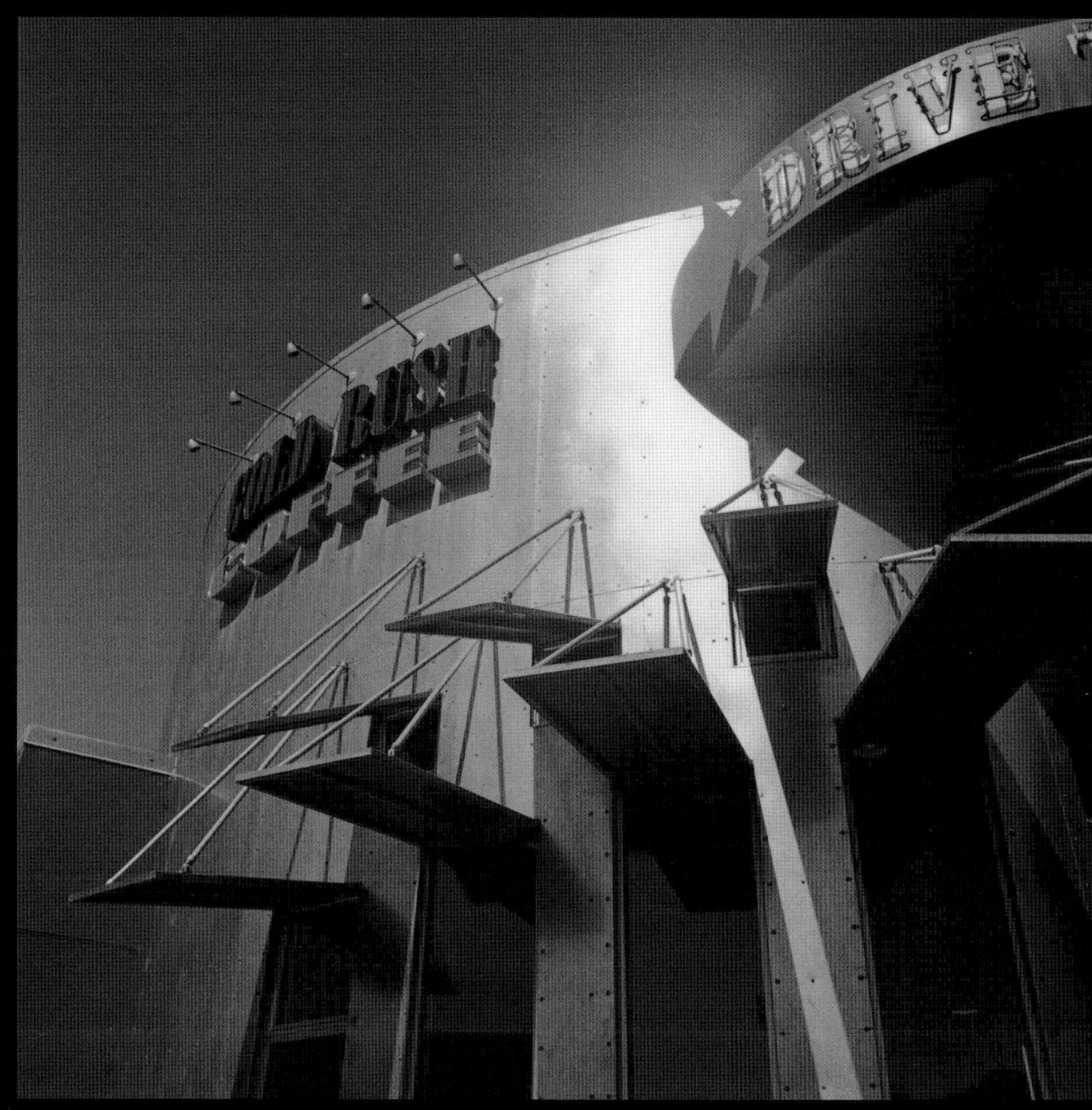
COFFEE
DRIVE

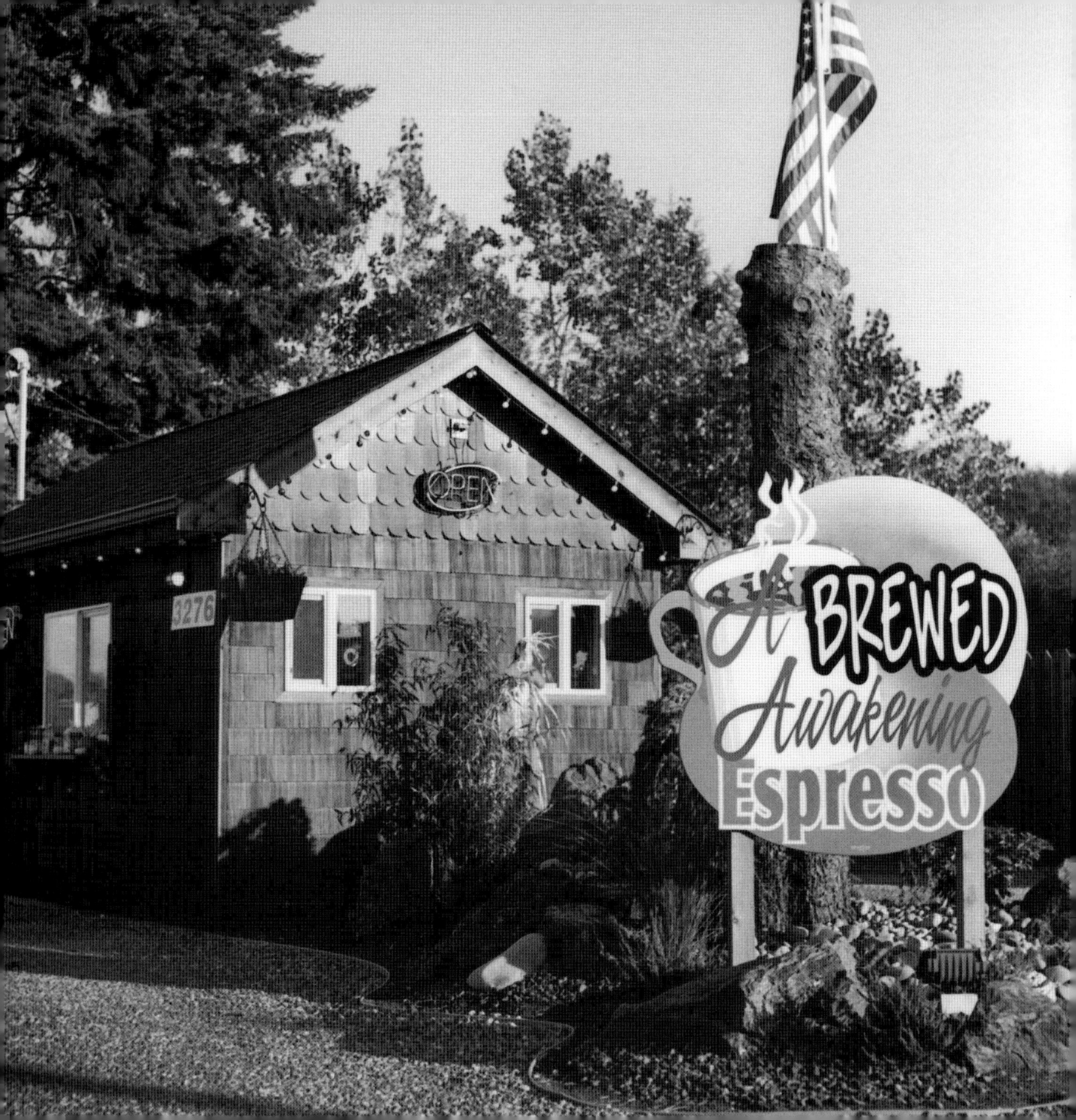
OPEN
3276
A BREWED
Awakening
Espresso

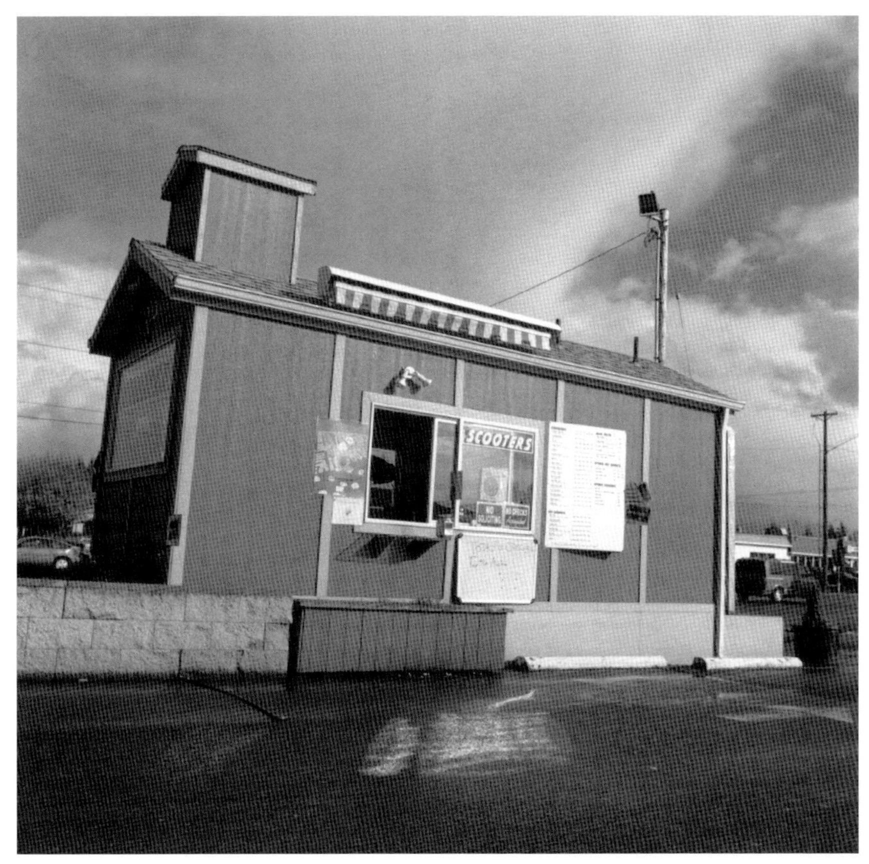

▲ *Scooters Coffee, Salem, Oregon*

◀ *A Brewed Awakening, Port Angeles, Washington*

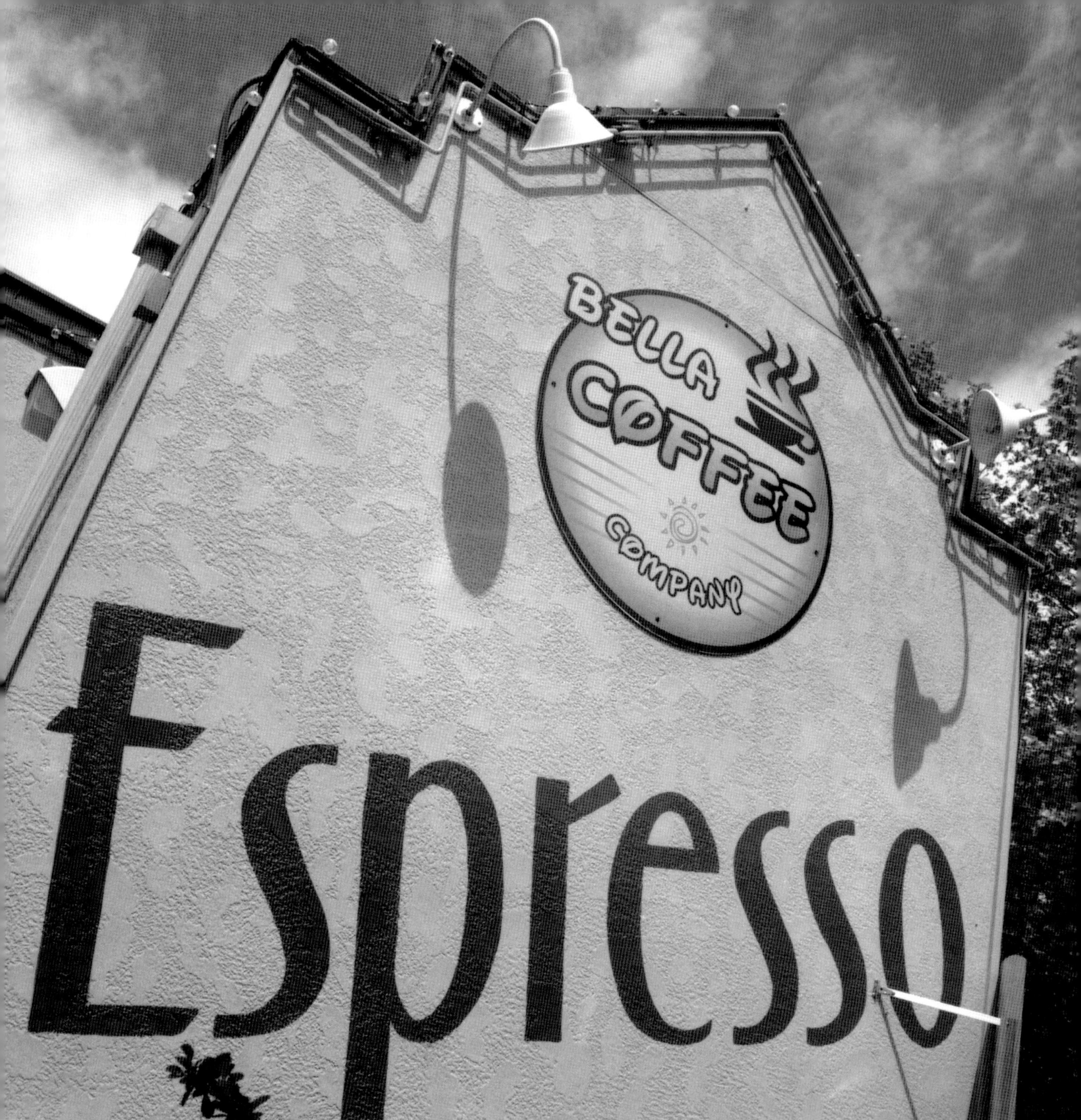
BELLA
COFFEE
COMPANY
Espresso

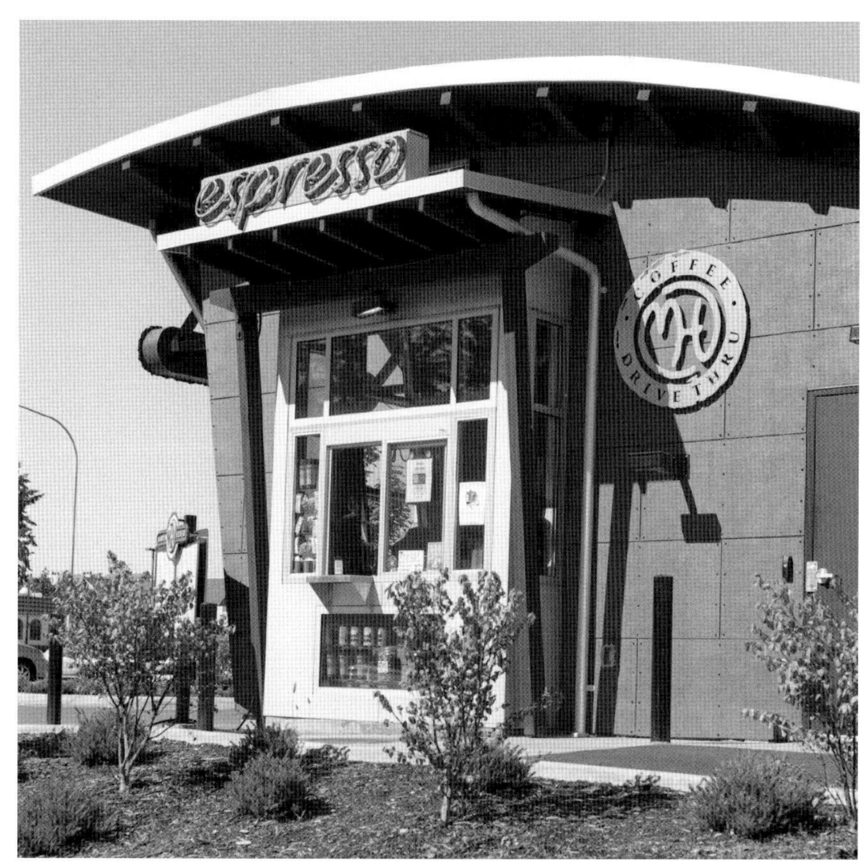

▲ *Martin Henry Coffee, South Hill, Washington*

◂ *Bella Coffee Company, Renton, Washington*

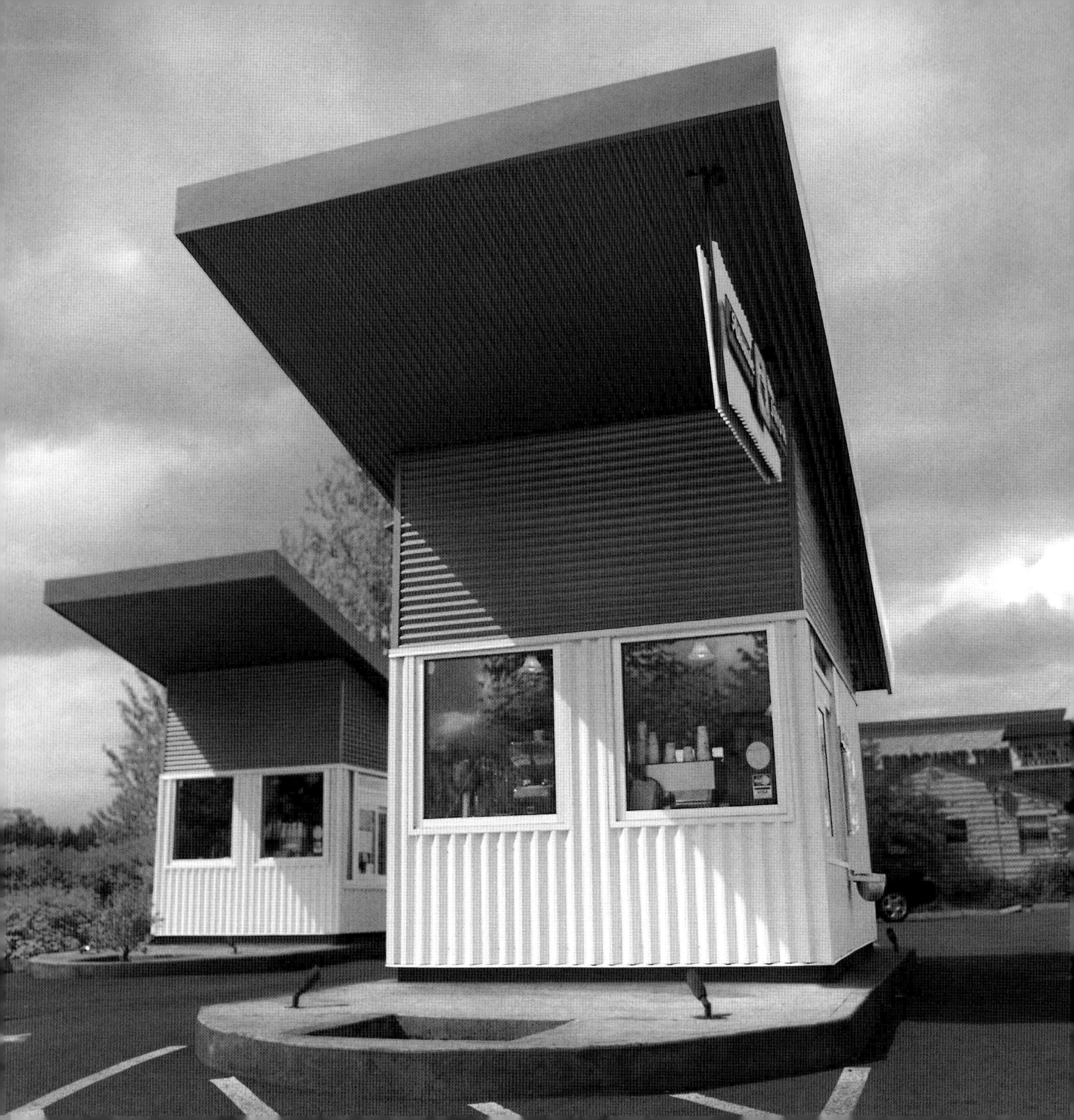

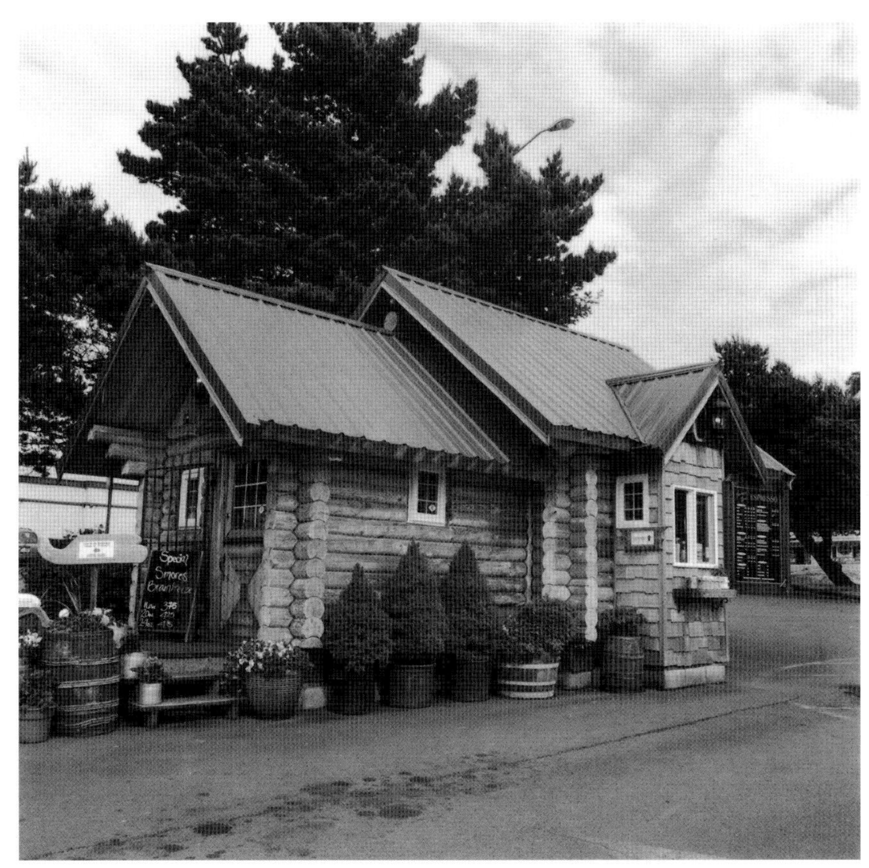

▲ *Journey's End, Astoria, Oregon*

◂ *Atomic Coffee, Bothell, Washington*

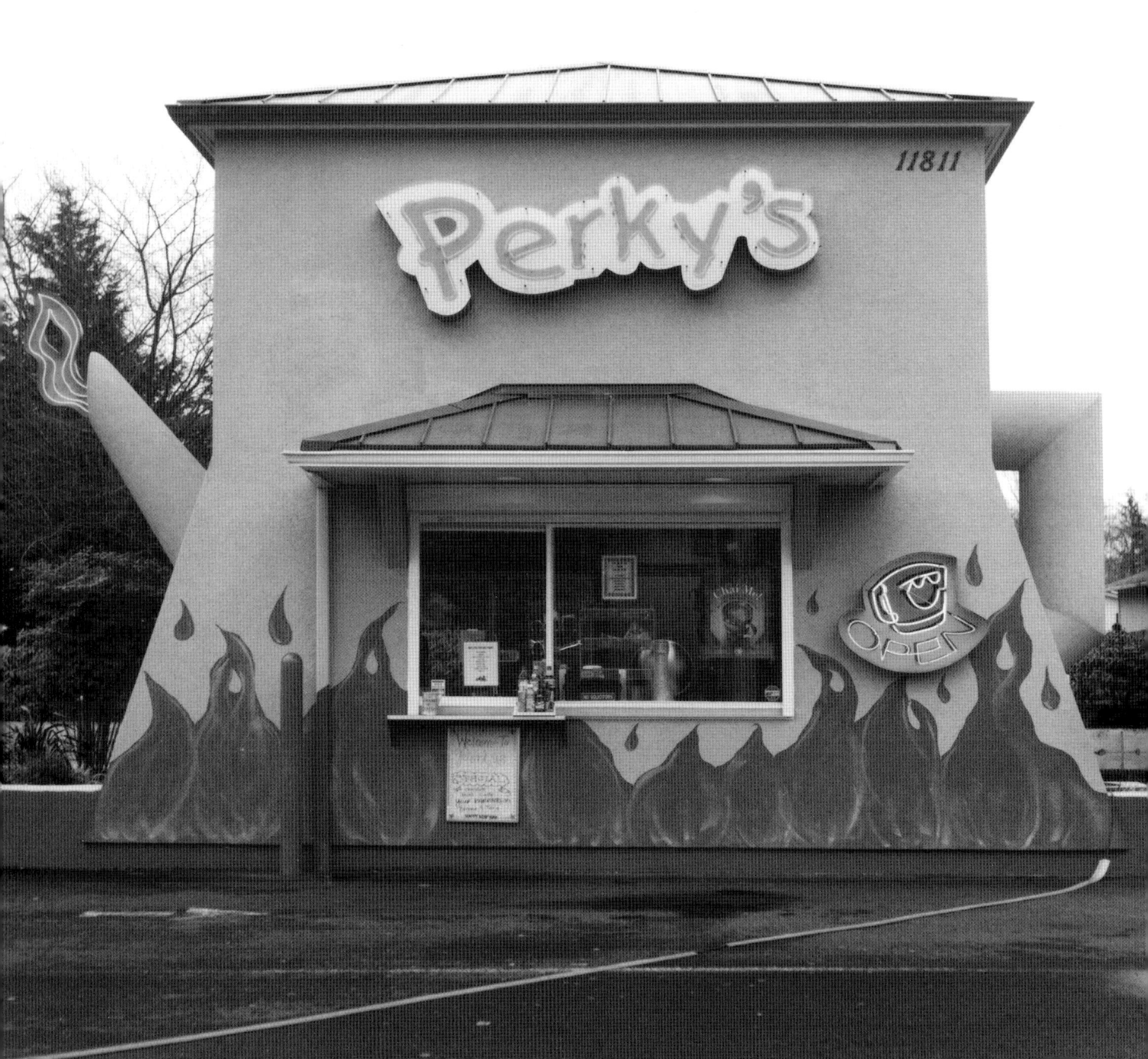
11811
Perky's
OPEN

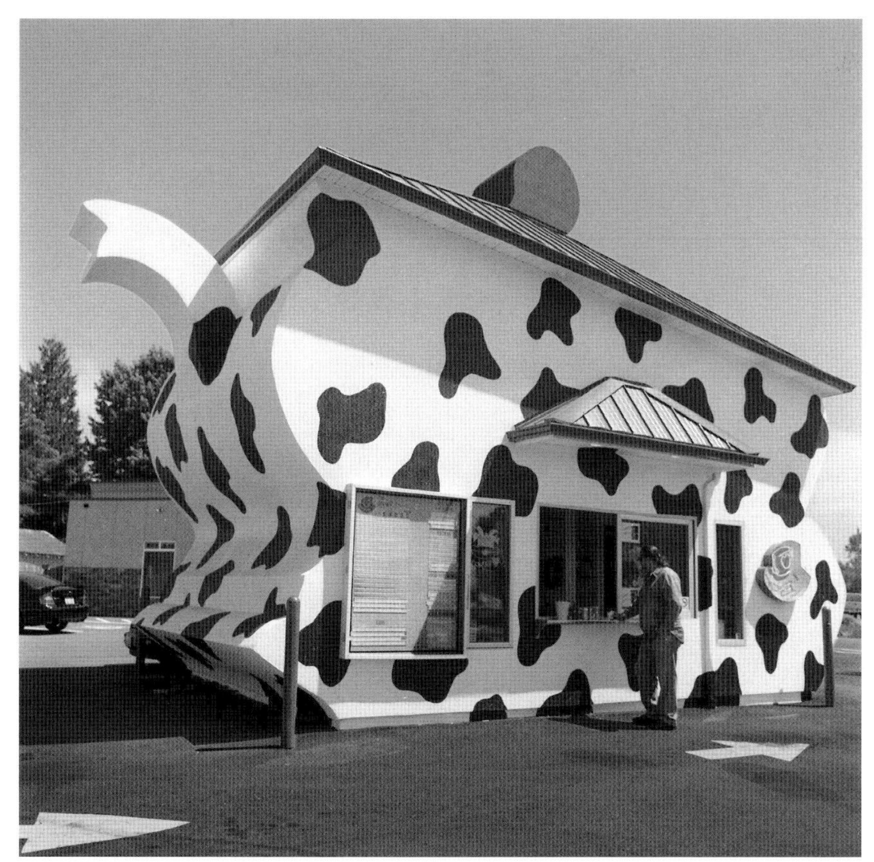

▲ *Cowgirls Espresso, Auburn, Washington*

◂ *Perky's, Puyallup, Washington*

Hotspot Coffee, *Arlington, Washington*

Hotspot Coffee's shiny aluminum stand is owned by the Berg family—Michael, Gabriel, and Ashley. Michael's design is trademarked and they employed 26 craftsmen to construct it. This amazing drive-through features a pulsating neon "knob" on top, a steam-spewing spout, and glowing red lights beneath its base that mimic an electric stove burner.

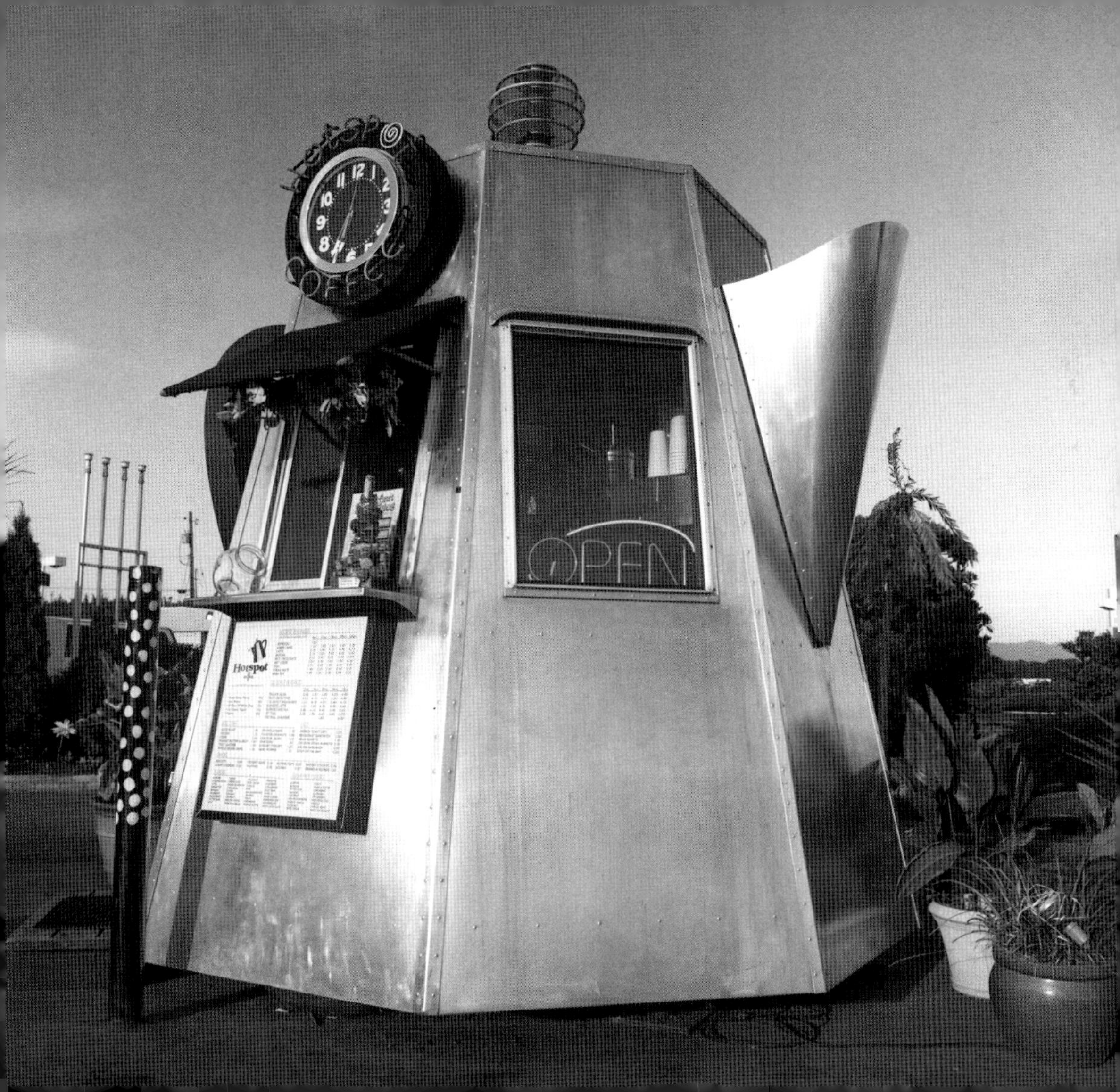
COFFEE
OPEN
Hotspot

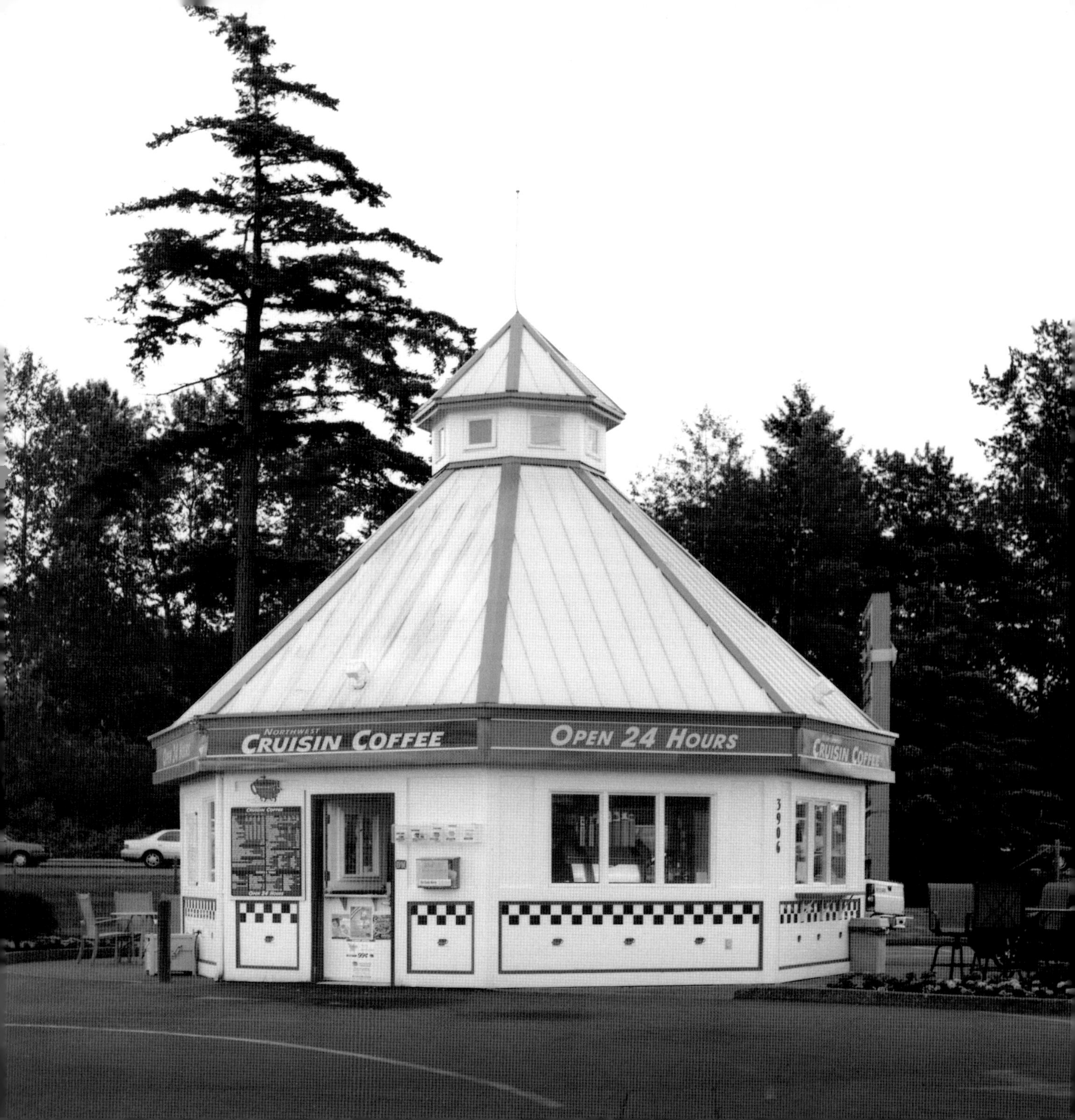
NORTHWEST
CRUISIN COFFEE
OPEN 24 HOURS
CRUISIN COFFEE
3906
CRUISIN COFFEE
OPEN 24 HOURS

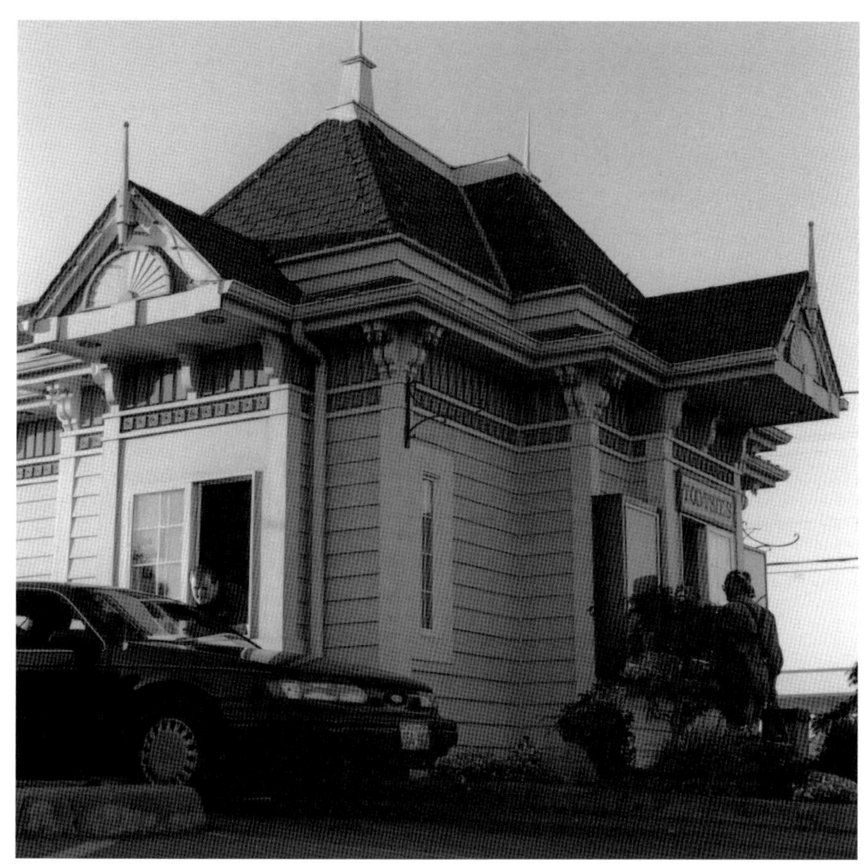

▲ *Tootsie's, Sequim, Washington*

◂ *Cruisin Coffee, Bellingham, Washington*

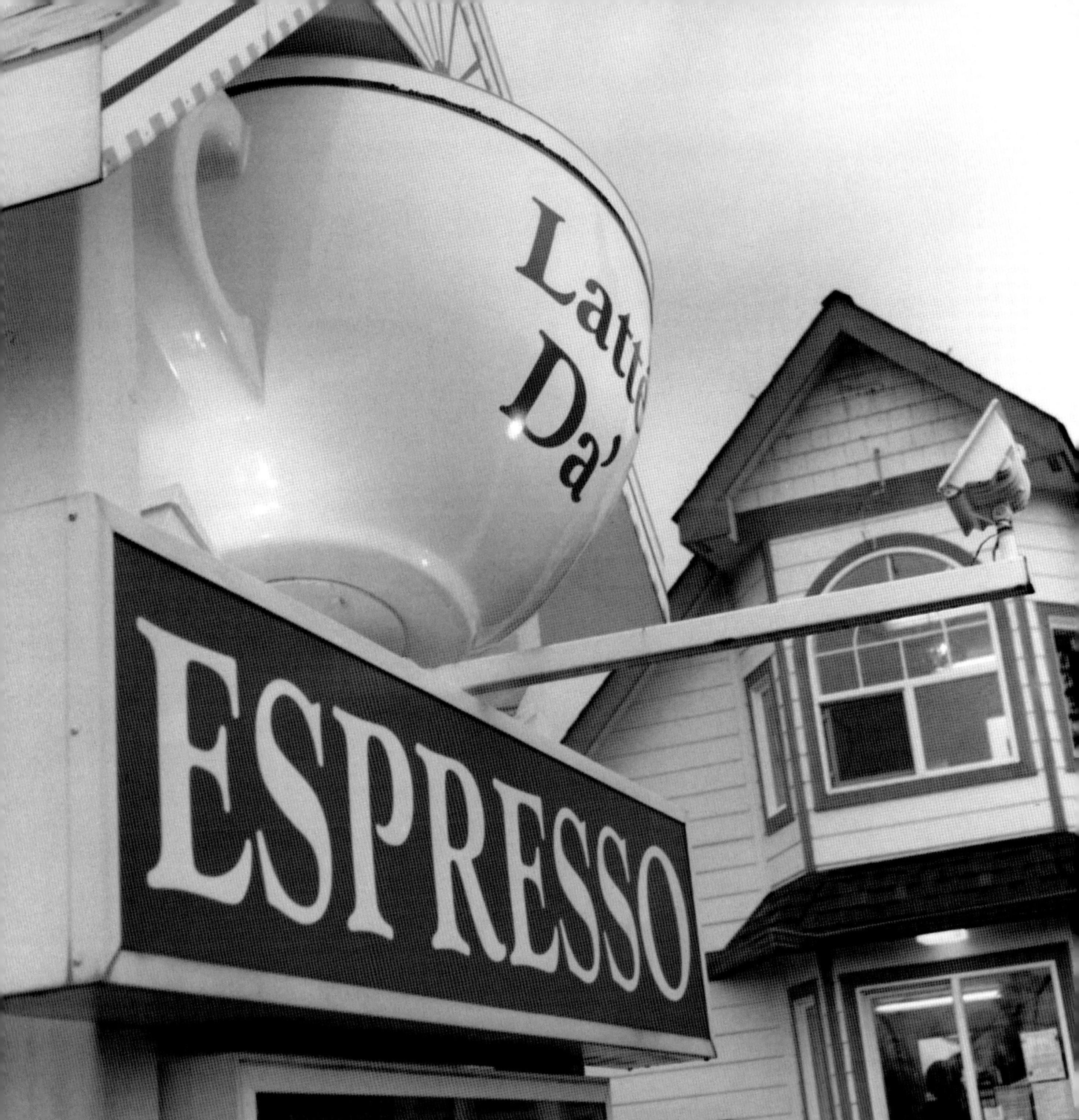
Latte
Da'
ESPRESSO

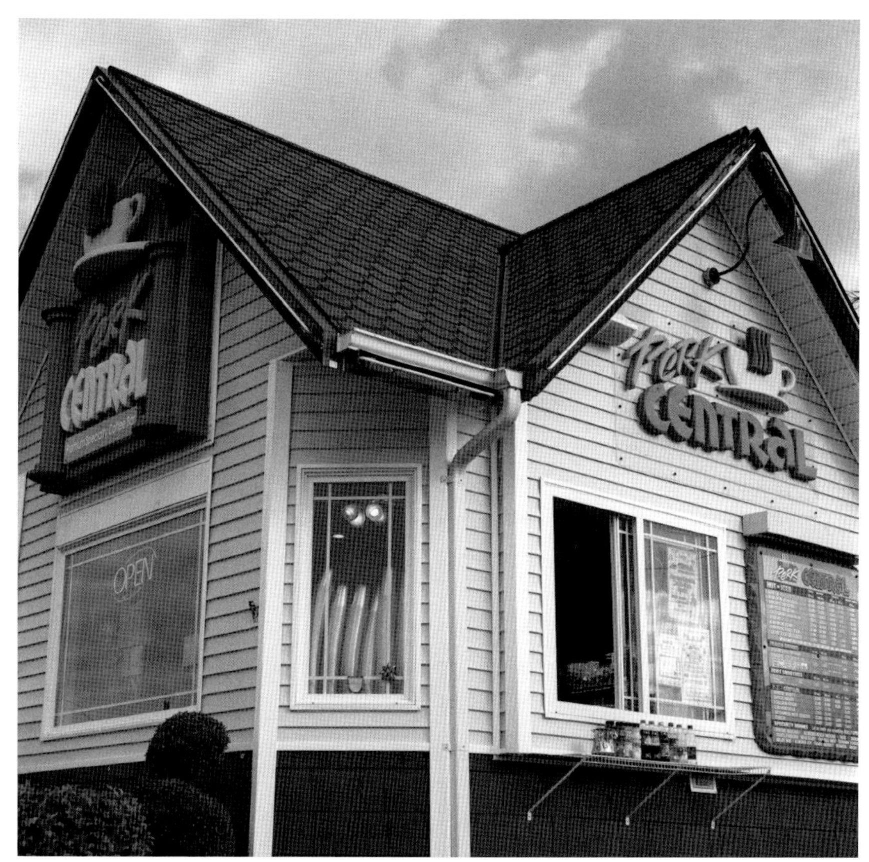

▲ *Perk Central, Lakewood, Washington*

◀ *Latté Da', Sedro-Woolley, Washington*

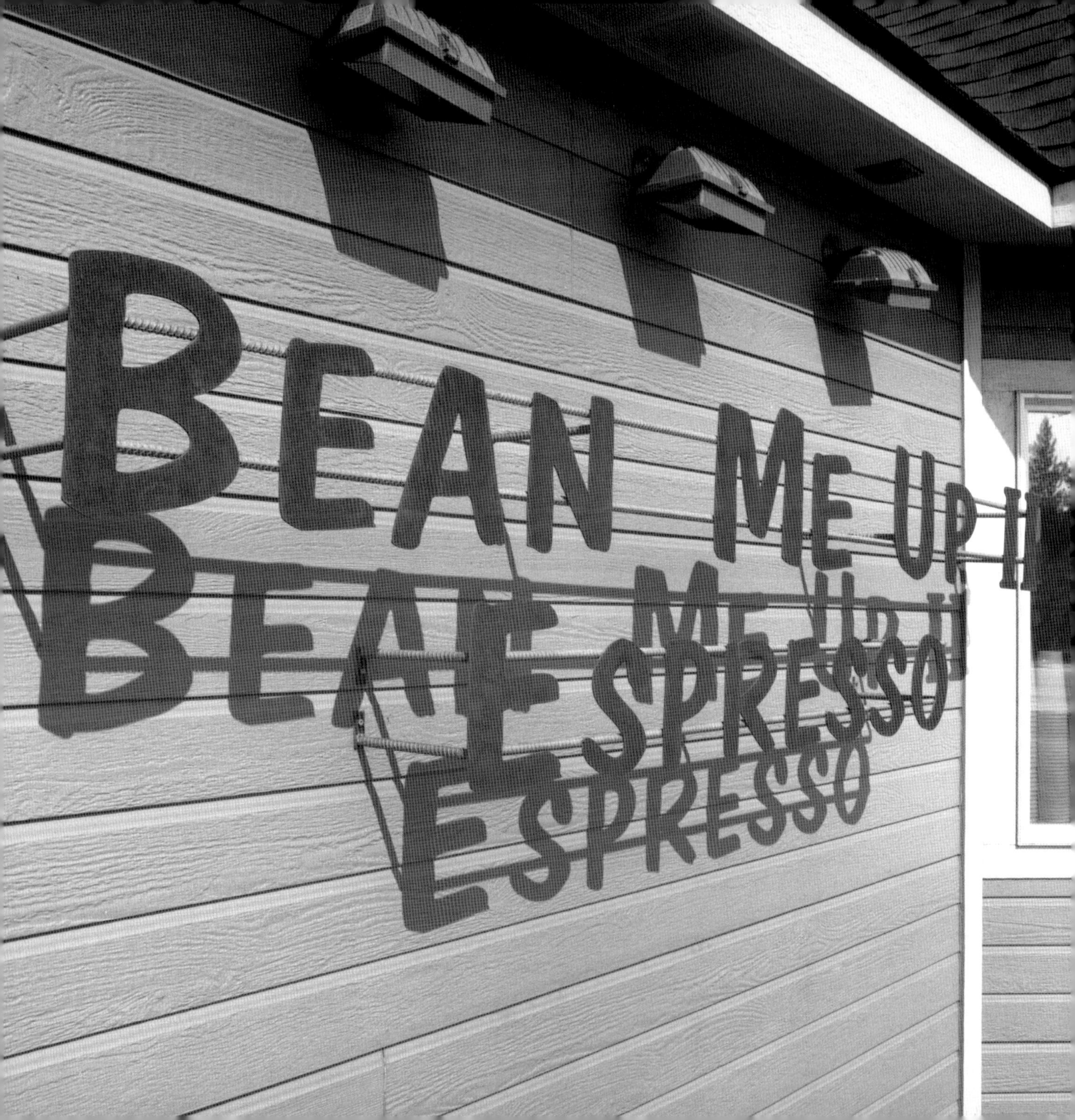
BEAN ME UP
ESPRESSO

▲ *The Bean Stop, Bellingham, Washington*

◄ *Bean Me Up Espresso, Spokane, Washington*

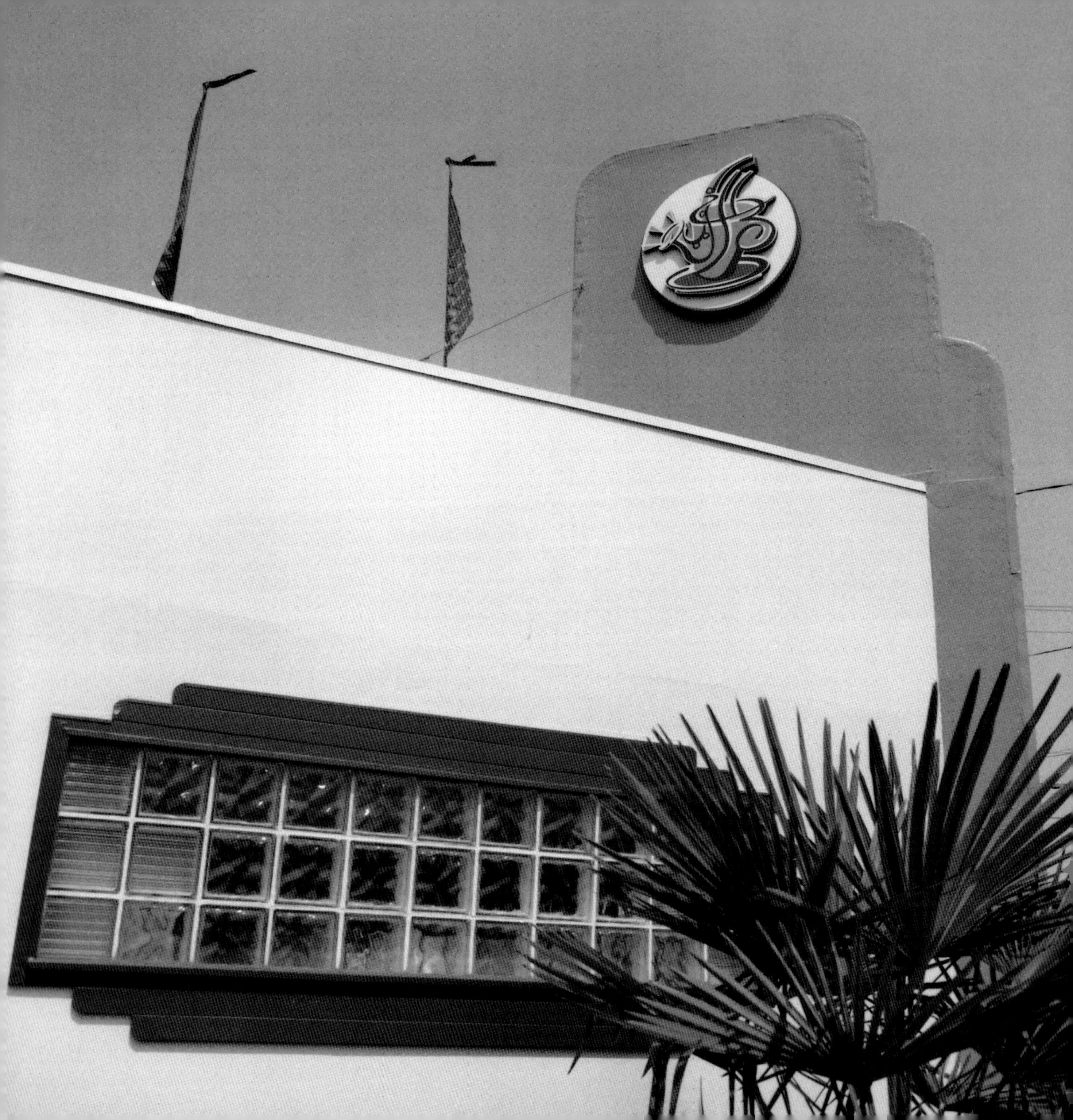

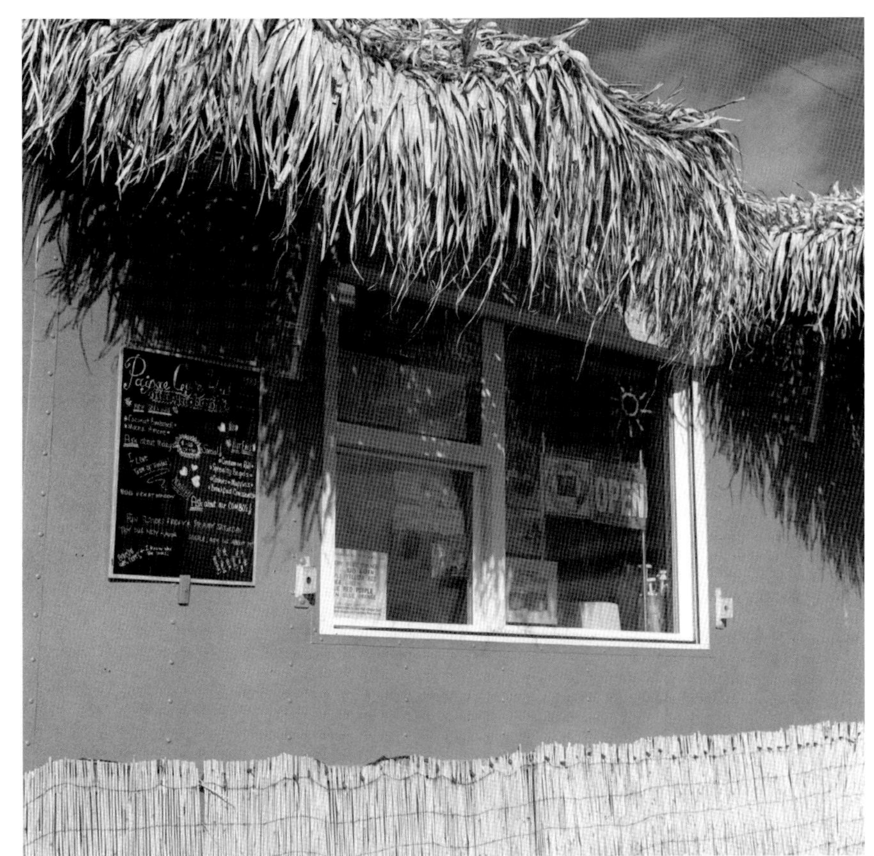

▲ *Paipea Cafe Hut, Tacoma, Washington*

◀ *Java Jazz, Seattle, Washington*

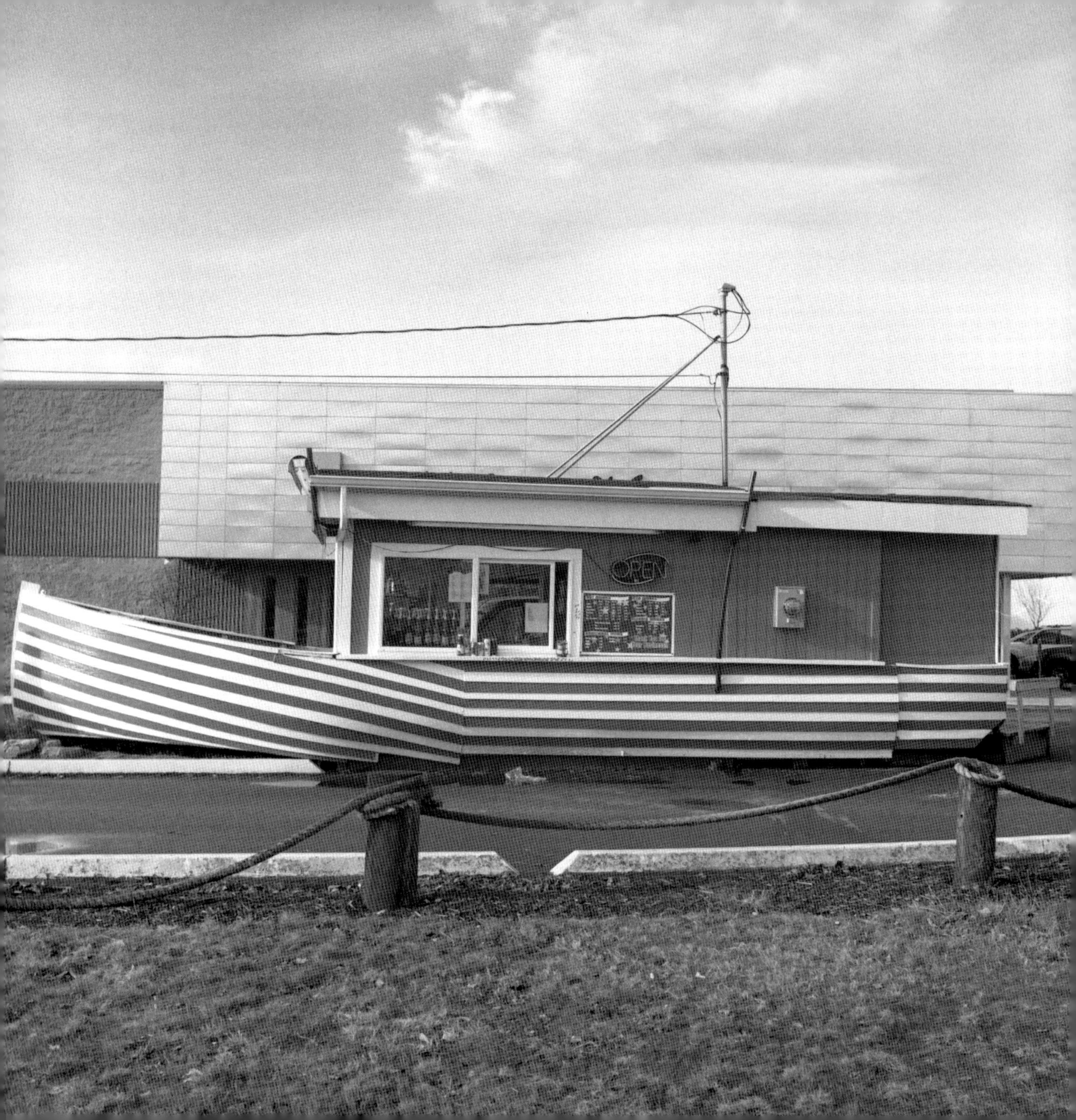
OPEN

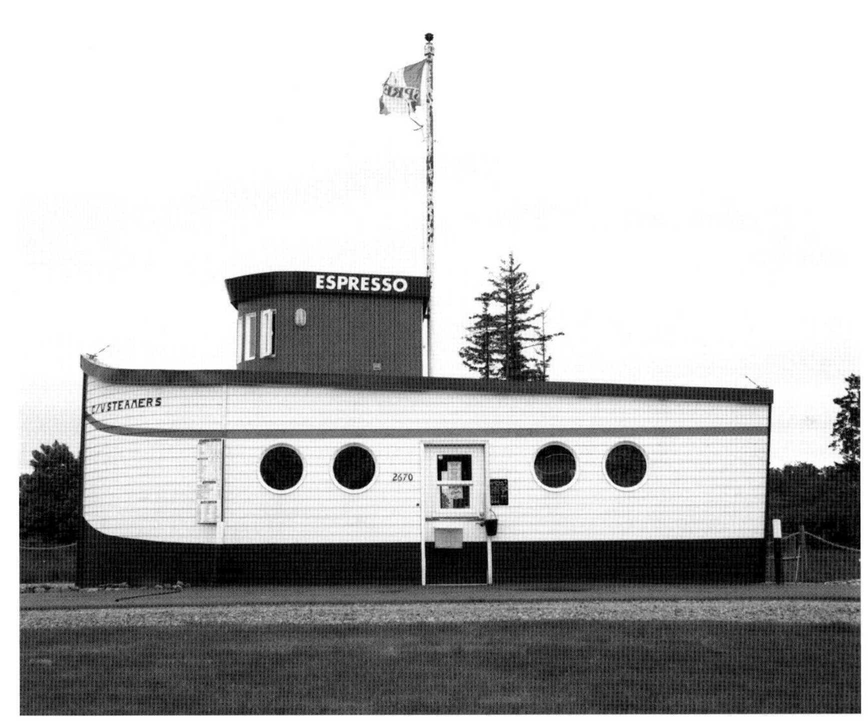

▲ *Steamers Espresso, Blaine, Washington*

◀ *Sunshine Espresso, Lynnwood, Washington*

The Jitter Bean Coffee Company, Eureka, California

The Jitter Bean is part of a small California chain that includes small- to medium-sized stands. This one blends in with the retro look of a nearby theater and is an adaptation of a diner the owners saw in a coffee-table book. The palm tree is a natural companion on the lot.

Palm trees are not abundant in the Northwest. Not real ones, that is. Nevertheless, artificial palm trees and tropical motifs are popular at many Northwest espresso drive-throughs.

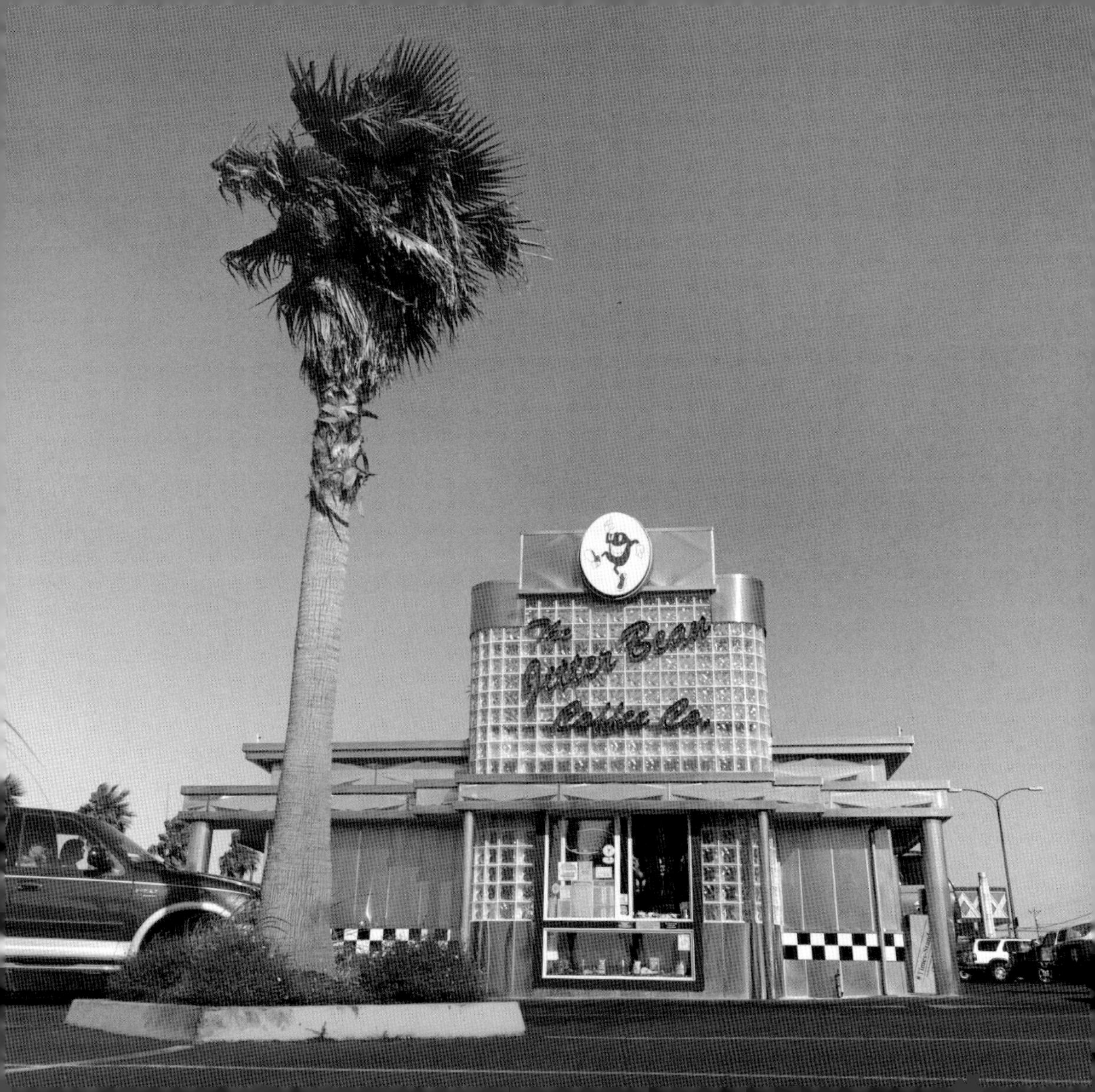
The
Jitter Bean
Coffee Co.

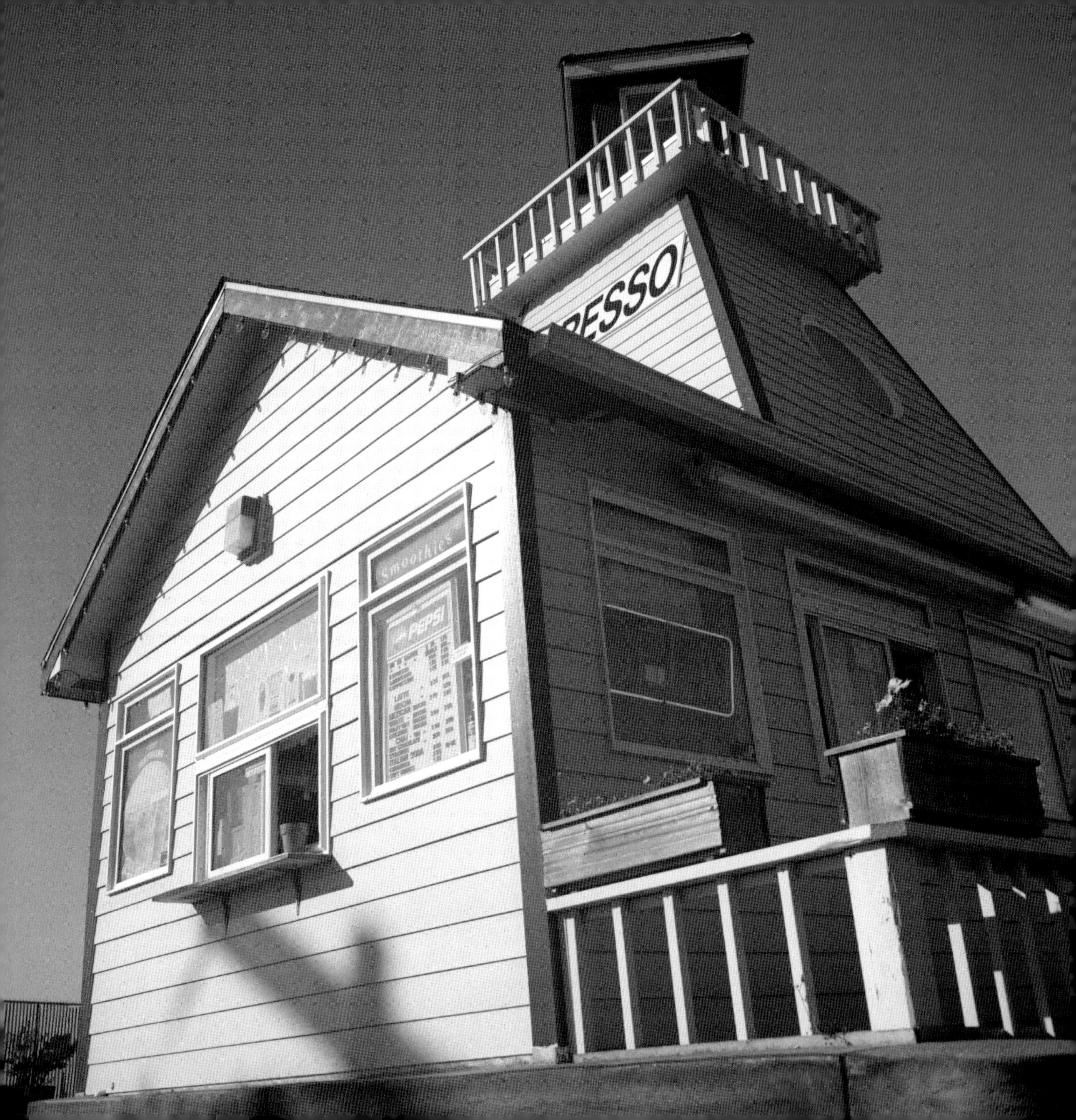
Smoothies
PEPSI

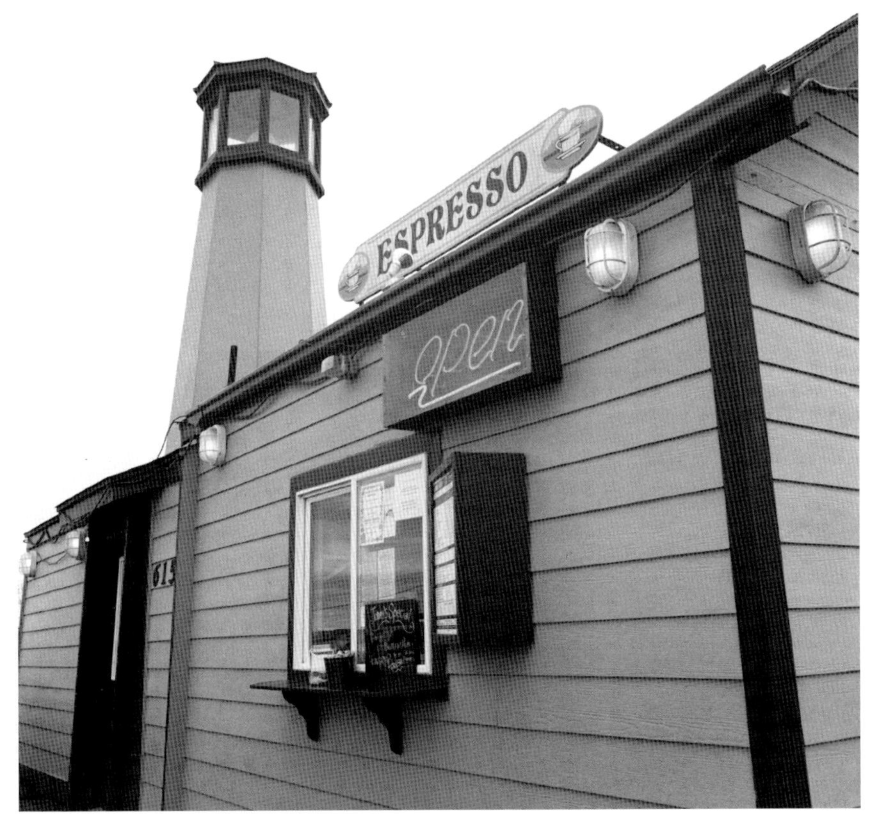

▲ *Latte 101 Espresso, Sequim, Washington*

◂ *Lighthouse Espresso, Lincoln City, Oregon*

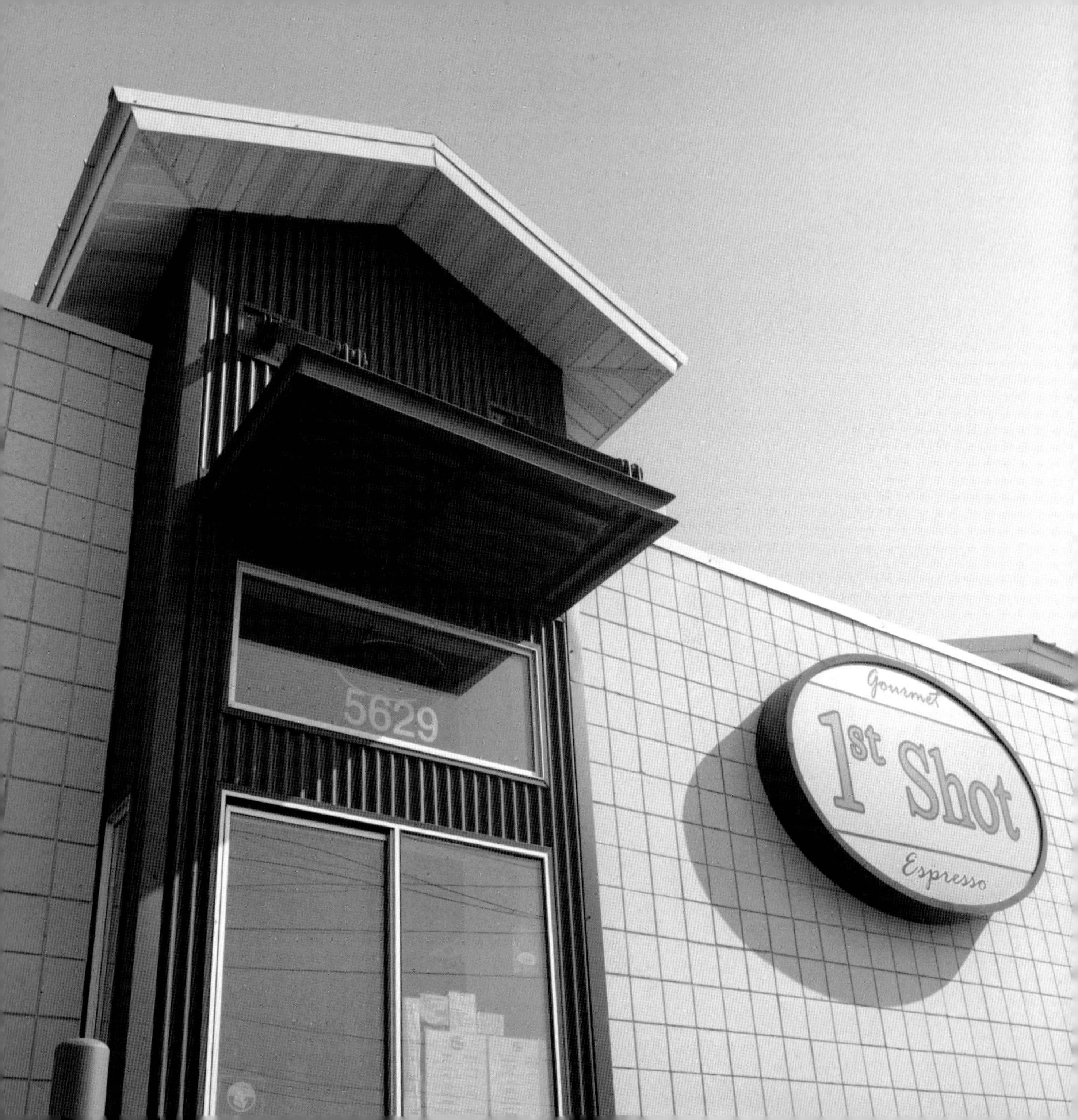
5629
Gourmet
1st Shot
Espresso

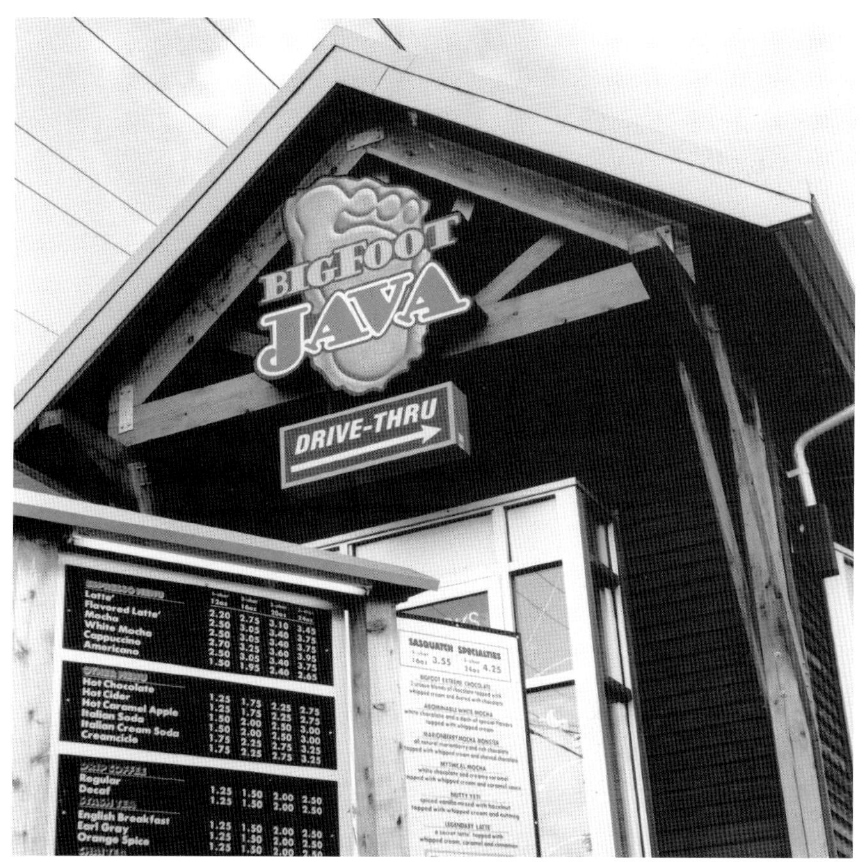

▲ *Big Foot Java, Everett, Washington*

◂ *1st Shot Espresso, Spokane Valley, Washington*

About the project

Several years ago I noticed, as everyone in the Northwest undoubtedly did, that espresso drive-throughs were popping up on nearly every arterial road and at most freeway on-ramps. What makes these drive-throughs stand out is not just the shere number of them, but that each one has its own personality—quirky in more ways than one. To this point, most are owned individually and are not products of the corporate world, which in this day and age makes them all the more interesting and wonderful.

These buildings need to be documented, not only because of their photogenic qualities, but also because the very nature of their ownership and operation makes them fragile in today's homogenized world.

These photographs were taken from 2004 to 2008 in the Pacific Northwest—from Eureka, California, to the Canadian border, and from the coast to Coeur d'Alene, Idaho. Over 200 coffee stands and carts were photographed, out of which 105 are included in this book.

The captions reflect the names of the businesses when they were photographed. In some cases, the names changed prior to publication, the buildings have been moved or destroyed, or the businesses have changed hands since they were photographed.

One of the facets of the businesses that escaped my lens was the creativity of the owners in naming them. They ranged from the straight-forward (Northwest Coffee Company) to the humorous (Bean Me Up Espresso) to the dramatic (Xtreme Caffeine). Coming up with a unique name is a challenge—the Washington State Department of Revenue has registered 8,439 business names that contain the words "espresso," "coffee, or "java."

About the photographer

Ray Weisgerber lives in Edmonds, Washington, just north of Seattle. He has a college degree in graphic design from the College of Design, Architecture, Art, and Planning at the University of Cincinnati, in his hometown. In addition to his long career in publishing as well as in the software industry, he has been building his photography skills for the past 40 years and has had photographs published in 11 books and magazines. He also regularly shows fine art photographs in galleries.

Beginning in the late 70s, Ray witnessed the entire evolution of Seattle's coffee culture, starting with sidewalk carts and the birth of the Starbucks phenomenon. While taking numerous driving tours of the Northwest, he has encountered hundreds of the independent coffee stands that became the subject of this book.

•

Technical notes: all images were created on film using a Mamiya C330 and a 55 mm or 80 mm lens. Scans were made from either prints or film negatives and tonal control was processed in Photoshop.

Thanks

Most of all, I want to thank my wife, Shirley, who waited patiently in the car on just about every car trip we took in the past several years. Even more importantly, she helped me realize that this project was worthy and doable.

In researching this book, I relied on some key insiders: Ed Arvidson, Robert Burgess, Christian Kar, Lon LaFlamme, Bruce Milletto, and Scott Olson. Their expert help was very much appreciated!

Thanks, also, to Bob Mullins and the whole gang at Moonphoto in Seattle who hand-processed all of my film with tender loving care. I am so thankful that there are still individuals who share my enthusiasm for quality black-and-white film photography.

Index

M

N

O

P

Q

R

S

T